Live Foods for the People
By Rainie Sunshine

Photography & Photo Art by Jeff Eichen

Rainie Sunshine's *Live Foods for the People* is a guide to increasing the color, crunch, and vibrancy of your diet, providing easy-to-follow recipes, ideas, and inspirations. Efficient and proficient, this book will satiate you and your family in style, comfort, and health.

Live foods are whole foods that have not been altered by high temperatures. Rainie Sunshine shares over 100 recipes and techniques to feed your desire for a diet that is more nutritious and more alive.

Rainie knows that you are what you eat. When you eat a diet that is rich in vitamins, minerals, and active enzymes, you become a more lively and vibrant being.

With over twenty years of experience creating healthy and delicious food and beverages for her community, Rainie Sunshine, the founder of Livin' Sunshine, has created this book as a nutritive and flavorful offering for people everywhere.

Photography & Photo art by:
Jeff Eichen of Rawmaste Productions and Goods
www.rawmaste.org

Graphic design for cover background and logo by:
Sarah Peller of Fruition Design
www.SarahPellerDesign.com

Edited by James Frazier

ISBN # 978-1-4675-5649-1

Self published with DiggyPOD
www.diggypod.com

Drawing on over twenty years of experience providing food and beverages for her community, Rainie Sunshine's *Live Foods for the People* is full of recipes that are easy to follow, using readily available, whole-food ingredients. Find delicous live dessert, sweet and savory bread, tortilla, calzone, cracker, pâté, salad, ferment, and beverage recipes within.

Live Foods for the People

By Rainie Sunshine

Photography & Photo Art by Jeff Eichen

❖

This book is dedicated to those who value

great food, great health, and great flavor.

…To the connoisseurs of vibrancy…

❖

Live Foods for the People Contents

❖

In my experience, balance will create
sustainable energy. Sustainable energy
means that your Raw Food Diet is not a
fad, phase, or fluke. Your Raw Food Diet
is you. It is not about being 100% Raw.
It is about a Raw Organic Food mindset
that is woven deeply and comfortably into
your life that is sustainable.
And totally satiable.

❖

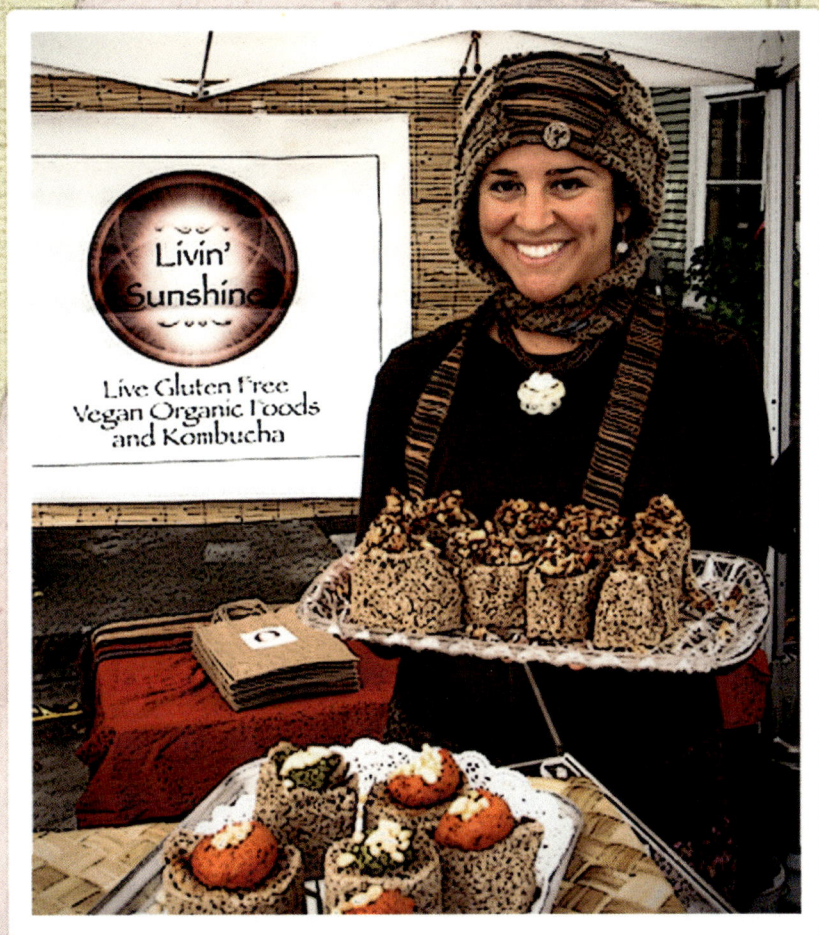

Livin' Sunshine

Live Gluten Free
Vegan Organic Foods
and Kombucha

The focus of this book is the preparation of live foods that satiate. Live foods are whole foods that have not been altered by high temperatures. Relative to cooked foods, they are less processed, more vibrant, and their nutrients are more available to the body. You will find that you need to eat less, while absorbing more energy. The flavors, health, and colors are bold expressions of life. The live food combinations found within not only satisfy your nutritional needs, but are also comforting, filling, fun, and delicious.

Every meal, every snack is an opportunity to eat something new, exciting, and fantastic. Let's face it: We love to eat great food. Not just healthy, not just organic, we want beautiful, colorful, exciting, and of course, totally delicious foods to fuel our amazing, dynamic lives.

This book and the recipes within are à la carte. They are meant to prepare you for the menu of the day. Personally, I am intimidated and frustrated by extensive and complicated recipes. Instead of spending hours in the kitchen making one meal, I would much rather spend those hours creating a variety of elements that can be easily combined to make a dozen meals. As a mother of two, I need to be practical *and* provide great food.

When *cooking* meals, it seems that it is enough just to have great ingredients on hand and, given an hour or two of preparation, we can create a complete meal. However, when we honor our body's desire to eat a predominately live food diet, there is often a lot more preparation needed. Some elements may take days to prepare.

For example, let's say it is Friday night and you want to make a pizza for the family. If you were to *bake* your pizza, you could put the dough to rise, and voilà, in an hour and a half, you would be enjoying your creation. You could also buy a premade crust, and bake your own in just half an hour. You could even have pizza delivered to your door! But, if you wanted a Live Cuisine Pizza you would need 24+ hours to make and dehydrate that crust. In *Live Foods for the People*, we are going to dive into the art of not only making this pizza crust, the savory spread, and the cashew-macadamia nut cheese, but we are going to create a map of the week, so that you are ready with the ingredients and the premade elements necessary to make this live pizza "on the fly," as they say in the restaurant kitchens where hungry people come in and need dinner in thirty minutes or less. Sometimes life moves that fast.

I suggest preparing the components of your meals in advance, so that when the busy-ness of life comes your way, you are already equipped with everything you need for sumptuous, live meals. One of the most common reasons that prevents people from eating a raw food diet is the amount of preparation involved. With this book, I hope to give you the feeling that your live food pantry is just as stocked as folks who have the luxury of getting their pantry items at the grocery store. We will identify the key items that can make a great week of food for your busy life, and make a plan for having those items on hand. Many grocery stores are beginning to carry more pre-made live food items. Unfortunately, very few of us can afford to have all of their crackers, breads, spreads, desserts, and soups made for them. Instead, we need to be empowered and inspired. We need to have great recipes and a great plan.

Don't let hunger or lack of preparation cause you to sacrifice your own wonderful health!

❖

100% Raw?

"Are you 100% Raw?" I reply, "I am 75% raw and loving it!"

As the chef and operator of a gourmet raw food booth at the popular Port Townsend, Washington, Saturday Farmer's Market, I heard this question again and again. Honestly, I try not to place much emphasis on strict percentages. I try to remain balanced and flowing as I go through my day's food journey. In my experience, balance and flow create sustainable energy. Sustainable energy means that your Raw Food Diet is not a fad, a phase, or a fluke. Your Raw Food Diet is you. It is not about being 100% anything. It is about a living food mindset that is woven deeply and comfortably into your being, and that is sustainable and totally satiable.

"75% raw and loving it" is such a great place to be. And believe me, it is a change from the standard way of eating. Picture a day in a household: a person wakes up and enjoys a breakfast of Earl Grey Tea, pasteurized orange juice, toast, and a light tofu scramble. Lunch is a grilled panini sandwich, an orange, and a stevia cola. For dinner, let's say this person has eggplant parmigiana with a salad. This is an example of how many people eat. Yes, without a doubt, it is far healthier than what most people are putting into their bodies every day. Yet, even if this vegetarian or vegan day was all organic, notice how cooked the meals are. This food is 75% cooked and only 25% live. I believe this ratio often leads to bloating, inflammation, and sluggishness over time.

For years, I was having similar daily food journeys. I was enjoying all organic health food, but I could sense a lack of vibrancy. I began to notice how "dead" many of my ingredients were: bread, pasta, rice, beans, crackers, etc. My grocery cart, and thus my body, were filled with these packaged, processed, and lifeless elements. The vegetables would, more often than not, get steamed, fried, or baked at temperatures that muted their vibrancy.   Fruit was often raw, but without the proper enzymes and minerals in my digestive system, the fructose was a source of sugar within an unbalanced diet.

I began to search for something new, and I found live foods. With the newfound knowledge of live cuisine, my grocery cart, and my body, are now more alive, more vibrant, and filled with the enzymes, minerals, and vitamins that I was lacking. Brimming with color, juiciness, crunch, and life, I began creating a new way of being. Let's take this new way of being and suppose a new day.

Within this new model, we wake up and enjoy a breakfast of yerba mate tea, a green smoothie, and a slice of live sprouted cranberry hazelnut bread with sweet, creamy cashew butter. Lunch is a sprouted mung bean salad with arame seaweed, live crackers with a live savory spread, and a quart of lemon water. Hmmm, for dinner, let's have sprouted nori rolls with a delicate miso soup. Aaah, finish with herbal tea and some bites of homemade raspberry torte, and we call it a day. This is quite a difference from the first day!

This is Raw and LOVING it. Now, our meals are full of lighter, living energy. At the end of a day like this, we can feel our center, and operate around that center, as we care for ourselves, our family, and our world. When our stomach, liver, kidneys, and intestines are so clogged, inflamed, bloated, and diseased by the overconsumption of cooked, dead, glutinous, unsprouted, grain-based heavy foods, we cannot feel our center.

So, if this Raw Food Diet is so great, why not 100% Raw?

I have tried to be 100% Raw. But when I tell myself that I cannot have any cooked foods, I instantly start craving them. Cravings run very deep. In her book, *12 Steps to Raw Foods: How to End Your Addiction to Cooked Food*, Victoria Boutenko talks about the chemical reaction that happens in the body when we consume cooked foods. This reaction can create feelings of intoxication, and can be powerfully addictive. These foods also have certain emotional relationships. For example, I feel soothed by starchy, high-fat combinations, remembering how, as a child, it felt great to be filled by rich foods such as bread and cheese, or fried potatoes. If I tell myself that I cannot have any of these foods, I go without for a while, but then end up bingeing on them, in a disappointing lapse in my wonderful raw way of being. By allowing myself up to, say, 30% cooked foods, I take care of my needs to feel free, creative, and intoxicated by oven-roasted vegetables from time to time. By avoiding the binge, I also avoid the unhealthy overload and guilt that is created by falling all the way off the wagon. By letting go of the "all or nothing" notion of being 100% Raw, I can also function comfortably at potlucks and restaurants.

By including a reasonable amount of cooked foods, we can celebrate the abundance of knowledge, recipes, chemistry, and life from around the world. We can eat without feeling guilty. We can have a diet that is as eclectic and diverse as this fabulous Earth. Let us savor the flavors. Let's say YES! Yes to more life, more beauty, more energy, more flavor, and more creativity. We are *adding* to our diet, not depriving or restricting ourselves. This is about better life: higher quality, higher vibrations, and higher health.

It is my hope that the following recipes serve as inspirations and useful guides as you explore your inner universe. I hope that your mouth wraps around these flavors and hugs them with great satisfaction. Dive in and find the beauty of the natural world around and within you. Blessed be you, the chef; blessed be you, the light; blessed be you, the universe.

Eating Raw supports farmers!

Have you ever seen raw foodists at a farmer's market? It is absolutely amazing, beautiful, and inspiring how much produce goes home with them! As live food eaters, instead of our staple foods being wheat and rice, we are filled with the wonderful beauty and bounty of local organic produce. With live soups, spreads, salads, and smoothies fueling our days, we will come home from market spilling over with delectable ingredients.

Order your seeds, nuts, and grains in bulk to reduce your trips to the grocery store. When you get to the store, don't wander through the pre-packaged foods area. You can travel straight to the bulk bins and the produce section. And just look at that grocery cart — so beautiful!

Never forget, you are what you eat. And you are fabulous!

A Special Note about Dehydration...

Many recipes within this book call for a dehydrator. You *can* use an oven, convection oven, toaster oven, or even a solar oven in lieu of a dehydrator. Simply set the oven to the temperature closest to the ideal 115°F (46°C). The time to create a finished product will vary. Place the items to be "baked" on a tray or mesh that allows for maximum air flow around your breads, cookies, crackers, etc. It is necessary to release the accumulated moisture in the oven every couple hours. Ideally, if possible, set the door slightly ajar to promote air circulation. Placing a small fan to blow air into this opening will help air circulation tremendously.

Parchment paper and Teflex sheets are available to hold food during dehydration. If you use Teflex, you will need to flip all of your creations halfway through the process. In addition, Teflex is made of Teflon, which is a chemical some people object to coming into contact with their food. If rotating and flipping your creations is inconvenient or impossible, or you want to avoid Teflon, I recommend using unbleached parchment paper, which I believe is the superior product.

Using parchment means that once you put your breads, crackers, and kale chips into your dehydrator or oven, you do not need to visit them again until they are finished drying. With Teflex, inevitably, the thickest center of your dehydrated recipes will still be quite moist several hours into dehydrating. Parchment paper is thin enough, and conducts both heat and air enough, that breads, crackers, and kale chips will dry thoroughly without any flip or rotation necessary. Parchment paper can also be reused several times before discarding.

Food Prep Synergies

When we go to our pantry or refrigerator for sustenance, we are bringing our nutritional, taste, texture, and temperature needs, and of course, our need to get the job done.

Some items are made daily, or nearly daily, in the raw food kitchen. The elements that are best fresh each day are the green smoothies, live soups, salads, and fresh juices. Some elements of the live food kitchen continually create themselves, such as kombucha, kimchi, and sprouts. Once a brew or ferment is finished, it's time to start the next. Ideally, we would recognize when the ferments are getting low, and begin the preparations for our next batch before the kitchen is out of kombucha, sauerkraut, or mung bean sprouts. Remember, being ready with the satiating elements of a full life is what keeps us smiling and evolving towards our highest selves.

Look at your schedule; find an opening. You can make one large opening, such as a Saturday morning, or it could be a few smaller openings, perhaps in the evenings. Now, fill this opening with an empowering kitchen prep session. I find it is most beneficial to truly commit to this session. Write "Kitchen" on your calendar and/or enter it into your digital calendar. This will be a special time that you have set aside for you and your family.

Use the days before this kitchen session to assemble your ingredients. Elements needing to be soaked can be assembled the night before (or that morning if you are having an evening kitchen session). You can grind your seeds the evening before a session. Fruits, vegetables, and greens can be washed and prepped for use beforehand.

Remember to prep yourself too. Go on a walk, stretch, and breathe before your kitchen session. Play great music. Clean as you go. Happy, healthy chefs make great food!

Soaking is amazing. Why? It commits you to making the desired recipe! It can be easy to hide from the responsibility of making foods when there are no ingredients that will spoil if you do not seize the moment. When the sprouts, seeds, or nuts are in water, you know that you need to work with them, or else they will go to waste. Kitchen incentive is a wonderful thing!

It is out of necessity that we be as efficient as possible. Within this short window, let's try to make as many crackers, chips, breads, desserts, and spreads as we can. I know it sounds daunting, but if you think about stacking functions and maximizing kitchen movements, you can do it!

Identify which kitchen ingredients, tools, and appliances are needed, and make as many foods as possible during your food prep window. For example, when I soak my grains and nuts to make sprouted live nut breads for the week, I am sure to make the sweet breads *and* the savory breads, while also making pizza crust and sprouted live cereal. This is called "stacking functions." I have one soaking bowl and one food processor; with these, I am going to make many different elements of fantastic nutrition, all in one session.

❖

Whether you are prepping food for a day at work, school, or a day off, it is all about pre-made. It is inefficient to make each recipe from scratch for its single need. Instead, try to think in terms of batches. Think about stocking up. After a food prep session, I like to look in the fridge, freezer, and pantry, and feel that I just went to a gourmet live food wholesale store and got amazing food for a sweet deal. When we choose to afford the cost of ingredients and time, we are blessed with a Live Food Café right in our homes.

I like to call this style *the art of à la carte*. Ferments, spreads, breads, crackers, chips, and desserts are all available to you. Every day you get to create the rainbow on your plate or in your to-go containers. You are the artist of your life!

> *When we afford the cost of ingredients and time, we are blessed with a Live Food Café right in our homes.*

Here is a list of food prep synergies. Make a few different creations at once. Use one element to augment the next, fulfilling your needs with minimal effort. Make the most out of the energy you spend in the kitchen.

Raise your glass of carrot juice. Let's toast to maximization and efficiency!

* ❖ Make sweet and savory breads at the same time. Simply make "Basic Bread," (see page 17) omitting the ingredients that make it sweet or savory. Divide the Basic Bread in half, and add the elements that give it the distinct flavor of sweet or savory.

* ❖ Make bread, tortillas, crackers, and pancakes in the same session.

* ❖ When making a spread, add some flax seeds, and make crackers as well.

* ❖ When you are making kale chips, enjoy an amazing kale salad before they go into the dehydrator.

* ❖ When making a cake or pie, save some of the filling and/or frosting in order to have a sweet butter on hand as a spread, or an ingredient to enrich a smoothie.

* ❖ Make two or three savory spreads at a time. Even better, double the batch and place one of them in the freezer! You will love yourself later.

* ❖ Cakes and pies freeze great. Place individual slices into the freezer for wholesome dessert options "on the fly."

❖ When soaking seeds and nuts for a recipe, soak a little extra and dry them for very satisfying snacks and salad additions

❖ We all know that cleaning food processors, blenders, and standing tabletop mixers is no fun, so let's get as many uses out of them as possible. For example, I recently made basil pesto, key lime pie, mac nut cookies, and grated carrots, and I only washed the food processor once!

How did I do this? I planned out my usage of the appliance. First, I made the key lime pie. Beginning with the crust, I made a double batch and converted half of it into mac nut cookie balls and four tartlettes, with the rest set aside for crust. Then, I made the key lime filling.

I figured the residual oil and avocado would only add to my pesto, and the residual sweetness or vanilla flavor would be covered up by the bold flavors of the fresh pesto. So, from key lime pie and cookies to basil pesto. Finally, I grated one pound of peeled carrots to have on hand for salads, wraps, etc. Four creations—one clean-up. That is what I call synergy!

❖ Sauerkraut and other ferments offer us another time and work saving opportunity. Before I put my shredded veggies in a container with salt to pound out their juices, I set some aside for my salad! So easy, so obvious, but truly profound how much time these little efficiencies can create in our lives.

❖

Sweet Live Breads do not leave you feeling bloated, inflamed, or craving more to fill the glutinous voids of conventional breads.

Your mouth will dance with flavor, and your body will dance with wholeness!

❖

SWEET BREADS

Jeff Eichler ©2012

These breads are so wonderful. The first recipe I ever used to create these breads and cookies came from Sergei and Vayla Boutenko in the Raw Family's fabulous un-cookbook *Eating Without Heating*. This recipe was the foundation for literally thousands of loaves for myself, my family, and my community. These breads are comprised of sprouted grains, soaked nuts, seeds and various fruits, veggies, herbs, and spices. They do not leave you feeling bloated, inflamed, or craving more to fill the glutinous voids of conventional breads. Your mouth will dance with flavor, and your body will dance with wholeness!

A Special Note about Nuts & Seeds...

There are a great variety of nuts, and they all dehydrate differently. Please experiment with the nuts in the following recipes, while knowing that walnuts and pecans take longer to dry. They absorb more water during soaking, whereas almonds, brazil nuts, and hazelnuts dry much faster, and have a crunchier texture when they finish.

Many nuts and seeds contain a digestive inhibitor. What does that mean? When nuts and seeds are not soaked and sprouted, it is very difficult or impossible for your body to reap their full nutritional benefits. Soaking these nuts enables the body to metabolize them much more efficiently.

Grind flax seeds with a dry blender or a clean coffee grinder.

Why do we grind our flax seeds fresh? As flours are stored ground and unrefrigerated, they oxidize and lose many of their benefits. The oils within these seeds and grains can actually go rancid and become toxic. Fresh is Best!

If there is an allergy to flax, substitute with chia or sesame.

Basic Bread

To make "Basic Bread," soak 1 cup of nuts (such as almonds, hazelnuts, brazil nuts, walnuts, or pecans) and 1 cup of raw whole grains in pure water for a minimum of 7 hours at room temperature. "Raw whole grains" in the following bread recipes can include buckwheat, rye, barley, wheat, spelt, and other grains. We are *germinating* these nuts and grains. We are rousing them from their dormant state and *transforming* them into sprouted grains with life and enzymes that allow us to digest them more completely. Do your soaking in a jar or mixing bowl covered with a cloth.

Once the grains and nuts have soaked, rinse them thoroughly in a colander. Place the rinsed nuts and grains in a food processor along with ½ cup of pure water. This mixture is too thick to successfully blend in a blender. Process this base until both the nuts and grains have been incorporated into a dough-like consistency. It is best to do this in batches that fit your appliance instead of overfilling. Using a spatula, transfer this dough into a large mixing bowl.

In your blender, place ½ cup of raisins, ¼ cup of olive oil, and ¼ cup of water, and blend thoroughly. I suggest the blender over the food processor here, because in the food processor, you will be left with sweet chunks of raisin. The blender will pulverize the raisins, making them available for texture and subtle sweetness. Pour this wet mix into the grain/nut mix. Next, add 1-2 cups of fresh ground flax seeds to the mix. Add a dash of sea salt, and mix well. This is Basic Bread. To this you will add different herbs, spices, fruits, and veggies to make distinctly flavorful combinations.

For all of the following bread recipes, the 1 cup loaves will dehydrate at 115° for approximately 26 hours, and the ⅓ cup cookies at 115° for approximately 22 hours. Freeze dehydrated breads that you will not use in the next week, and store the rest in the refrigerator in an air-tight container.

Hazelnut Cranberry Sprouted Live Bread

1 Cup Raw Buckwheat Groats or other Raw Grains
1 Cup Raw Hazelnuts
1-2 Cups Fresh Ground Flax Seeds
½ Cup Raisins
¼ Cup Olive Oil
½ + ¼ Cup Water
⅓ Cup Honey, Agave Nectar, or Coconut Palm Syrup
1 Cup Juice Sweetened Cranberries
1 Tbsp Orange Zest
1 tsp Sea Salt
1 tsp Cinnamon   **Yields: 4-5 Large Loaves**
1 tsp Nutmeg   **or 12 Smaller Cookies**

Soak the grains and hazelnuts for at least 7 hours. Once the grains and nuts have soaked, place them in a colander (make sure the holes are small enough that you don't lose the grains) and rinse. Preheat your dehydrator to 115°. The grains and nuts are ready for the food processor, but take care not to overfill. It is best to do this in batches that fit your appliance instead of overfilling. While the processor is running, add ½ cup of water. When the grains and nuts are well combined, use a spatula to transfer them to a large mixing bowl.

In a blender, place the raisins, olive oil, and remaining water, and blend very well. Pour this mixture over the grains and nuts in the mixing bowl. Now, add the freshly ground flax seeds (between 1 and 2 cups, adding enough to bind the dough), sea salt, spices, and sweetener. Mix very well. Last but not least, fold in the beautiful red cranberries.

Use measuring cups to create uniform-sized loaves. Scoop 1 cup of the bread dough on to your dehydrator tray lined with parchment paper. Shape into an attractive loaf, and repeat. You can also use a ⅓ measuring cup to scoop the dough and shape into cookies. Dehydrate loaves for 26 hours, or cookies for 22 hours, at 115°.

Carrot Raisin Sprouted Live Bread

1 Cup Raw Nuts
1 Cup Raw Buckwheat Groats or other Raw Grains
1-2 Cups Fresh Ground Flax Seeds
½ + ½ Cup Raisins
¼ Cup Olive Oil
½ + ¼ Cup Water
⅓ Cup Honey, Agave Nectar, or Coconut Palm Syrup
2 Tbsp Molasses
1 Grated Medium Carrot (about 1 cup)
1 tsp Sea Salt
1 tsp Ground Nutmeg   **Yields: 4-5 Large Loaves**
2 tsp Cinnamon   **or 12 Smaller Cookies**

Soak the buckwheat and nuts for at least 7 hours. When your soak is complete, you're ready to make bread. Preheat your dehydrator to 115°. Place the grated carrot and ½ cup raisins into a bowl. Add the cinnamon and nutmeg, and pour the sweeteners over. Mix them together and add a splash of water if needed. Allow them to marinate.

Next, rinse the soaked nuts and grains, and place them into the food processor. While the processor is running, add ½ cup of water. Once the grains and nuts are well combined, transfer them to a large mixing bowl.

In a blender, place the other ½ cup raisins, olive oil, and remaining water, and blend well. Pour this mixture into the dough. Now, add the freshly ground flax seeds (between 1 and 2 cups, enough to bind the dough), and sea salt. Mix well. Finally, fold in the marinated carrots and raisins.

Now, create your loaves and/or cookies. 1 cup of dough placed on your dehydrator tray lined with parchment paper can be shaped into a loaf, and ⅓ cup of dough can be shaped into a cookie. The loaves will dehydrate at 115° for 26 hours, and the cookies at 115° for 22 hours.

Sprouted Live Banana Nut Bread

1 Cup Raw Pecans or Walnuts
1 Cup Raw Buckwheat Groats or other Raw Grains
1-2 Cups Fresh Ground Flax Seeds
½ Cup Raisins
¼ Cup Olive Oil
½ + ¼ Cups Water
⅓ Cup Honey, Agave Nectar, or Coconut Palm Syrup
½ Tbsp Sea Salt
3 Large Sliced Bananas   **Yields: 4-5 Large Loaves**
1 Tbsp Cinnamon   **or 12 Smaller Cookies**

Soak the grains and nuts for at least 7 hours. Once the grains and nuts have soaked, place them in a colander with small holes, and rinse well. Preheat your dehydrator to 115°. Set aside a few nuts to adorn each loaf or cookie before they go into the dehydrator. Transfer the soaked grains and nuts into the food processor, taking care not to overfill. It is best to do this in batches that fit your appliance. While the processor is running, add ½ cup of water. Once the grains and nuts are well combined, transfer them to a large mixing bowl.

Place the raisins, olive oil, and remaining water in a blender, and blend well. Pour this mixture over the grains and nuts in the mixing bowl. Add the freshly ground flax seeds (between 1 and 2 cups, adding enough to bind the dough), sea salt, cinnamon, and sweetener. Mix very well. Finally, fold in the sliced bananas. Set aside a few sliced bananas to adorn your loaves just before they go into the dehydrator.

Create uniform-sized loaves using measuring cups. Place 1 cup scoops of the bread dough on your dehydrator tray lined with parchment paper, and shape into attractive loaves. ⅓ cups can be shaped into cookies. Adorn with sliced bananas and soaked nuts. Dehydrate loaves for 26 hours, and cookies for 22 hours, at 115°.

Sprouted Live Blueberry Pecan Bread

1 Cup Raw Pecans (Other nuts may be substituted)
1 Cup Raw Buckwheat Groats or other Raw Grains
1-2 Cups Fresh Ground Flax Seeds
½ Cup Raisins
¼ Cup Olive Oil
½ + ¼ Cup Water
⅓ Cup Honey, Agave Nectar, or Coconut Palm Syrup
½ Tbsp Sea Salt   **Yields: 4-5 Large Loaves**
1 Tbsp Cinnamon   **or 12 Smaller Cookies**
1 ½ Cup Frozen or Fresh Blueberries (*Note: If you need to use dried berries, soak for 4 hours in warm water to reconstitute.*)

Soak the grains and pecans for at least 7 hours. When the soak is complete, place them in a colander and rinse well. Preheat your dehydrator to 115°. Set aside a few pecans to use as adornment for each loaf or cookie just before the breads go into the dehydrator. Transfer the grains and nuts to the food processor, taking care not to overfill. It is best to do this in batches that fit your appliance. While the processor is running, add ½ cup of water. Once the grains and nuts are well combined, transfer them to a large mixing bowl.

In a blender, place the raisins, olive oil, and remaining water, and blend very well to get the raisins fully blended. Pour this mixture over the grains and nuts in the mixing bowl. Now, add the freshly ground flax seeds (between 1 and 2 cups, adding enough to bind the dough), sea salt, cinnamon, and sweetener. Mix very well. Finally, fold in the blueberries.

Create your breads using measuring cups. 1 cup scoops can be shaped into attractive loaves, and ⅓ cups of dough can become convenient cookies. Place one or more of the pecans you set aside on top of your breads. Dehydrate loaves on parchment paper for 26 hours, and cookies for 22 hours, at 115°.

Cinnamon Raisin Sprouted Live Bread

1 Cup Raw Nuts
1 Cup Raw Buckwheat Groats or other Raw Grains
1-2 Cups Fresh Ground Flax Seeds
½ + ½ Cup Raisins
¼ Cup Olive Oil
½ + ¼ Cup Water
⅓ Cup Honey, Agave Nectar, or Coconut Palm Syrup
½ Tbsp Sea Salt   **Yields: 4-5 Large Loaves**
2 tsp Cinnamon   **or 12 Smaller Cookies**

Soak the grains and nuts for at least 7 hours. When the soak is complete, strain and rinse the nuts and grains. It is best to use a colander that has relatively small holes or a sieve, so that you don't lose too much grain through the holes during straining and rinsing. Preheat your dehydrator to 115°.

Next, place the nuts and grains in a food processor and blend well, adding ½ cup of water gradually. It is best to do this in batches that fit your appliance, instead of overfilling. Once the nuts and grains have combined, transfer the mixture into a large mixing bowl. Add ½ cup raisins, ¼ cup olive oil, and the remaining ¼ cup of water to your blender. Blend the raisins as smooth as possible; the mixture should look something like a salad dressing. Pour the mixture and the freshly ground flax seeds (between 1 and 2 cups, adding enough to bind the dough) into the dough. Now mix everything very well.   The ground flax seed is a binder and makes the bread able to shape. Finally, add the remaining ingredients: whole raisins, sea salt, cinnamon, and sweetener.

We are now ready to scoop and shape 1 cup loaves and/or ⅓ cup cookies on dehydrator trays lined with parchment paper. The loaves will dehydrate at 115° for 26 hours, and the cookies at 115° for 22 hours.

Sprouted Live Pancakes

Here's a live treat that will make a believer out of anyone.

Any of the previous recipes can be used to make Sprouted Live Pancakes. Choose which recipe you would like to use and make your bread dough. Now, instead of shaping this dough into ⅓ cup cookies or 1 cup loaves, let's shape them into beautiful pancakes. Place ⅓ cup of dough onto unbleached parchment paper on your dehydrator tray. Using your hands or spatula, spread the dough into a circle approximately ¼ inch thick. Take care to smooth the edges of your pancake.

Each recipe yields 12 lovely pancakes.

This is best if done at night because you can place them into the dehydrator just before bed, and wake up to amazing warm pancakes in the morning. Top these delicious pancakes with organic raw honey, fresh fruit, or maple syrup. Enjoy them after your green smoothie, tea, and a nice walk or yoga session.

Sprouted Live Cinnamon Rolls

2 Cups Raw Nuts
1 Cup Raw Buckwheat Groats or Other Raw Grains
1-2 Cups Fresh Ground Flax Seeds
½ + ½ Cup Raisins
¼ Cup Olive Oil
½ + ¼ Cup Water
⅓ + ⅓ Cup Honey, Agave Nectar, or Coconut Palm Syrup
½ Tbsp + a Pinch Sea Salt
2 + 2 tsp Cinnamon   **Yields 4-5 Cinnamon Rolls**

Place your nuts and grains to soak <u>separately</u> on the countertop overnight. After a minimum of 7 hours soaking, strain the nuts and grains, again <u>separately</u>. Rinse them very well using a colander. Preheat your dehydrator to 115°. Next, place 1 cup nuts and the grains in a food processor or blender with ½ cup of water and blend well. It is best to do this in batches that fit your appliance. Do not overfill it and compromise your ability to get a dough-like consistency. Once the nuts and grains have combined, transfer the mixture into a large mixing bowl.

Place ½ cup raisins, ¼ cup olive oil, and the remaining ¼ of water in your blender, and blend well. Pour the mixture into the dough and incorporate this moistening element into the dough. Over the top of this wet mixture, pour the freshly ground flax seeds (between 1 and 2 cups, adding enough to bind the dough). Mix very well. You can see how the flax seeds binds the ingredients together, making it shapeable. Now, add ½ Tbsp sea salt, 2 tsp cinnamon, and ⅓ cup of sweetener, and combine.

We are now ready to shape. First, spread your dough out on your unbleached parchment paper in a 10" x 10" square. I recommend a spatula for this. The dough should be about ⅓ inch thick and very even. Set this aside for the moment.

To prepare the filling, begin by placing the remaining ½ cup nuts, ½ cup raisins, a pinch of sea salt, 2 tsp. cinnamon, and ⅓ cup of sweetener into your blender or food processor. Blend into a paste. Using your spatula, spread this sweet paste evenly down one of the edges of the dough, in a strip about two inches wide. Now, using the parchment paper to help you get started, roll the entire bread like a sushi roll, beginning with the paste. Allow the parchment to separate from the roll once the bread is rolling onto itself. Wet or oiled hands will help shape and hold this together.

Slice this large roll into 3" sections, top with remaining ½ cup soaked nuts. These are your gorgeous cinnamon rolls! Dehydrate for about 22 hours at 115°.

Top finished rolls with a **Macadamia Nut Glaze**:
1 Cup Macadamia Nuts
⅓ Cup Agave Nectar, Raw Honey, or Coconut Palm Syrup
Pinch of Sea Salt
⅓ Cup Nut Milk
A touch of Vanilla

Blend until impeccably smooth. Drizzle over and ENJOY!

The following sunflower seed recipes yield 25 1-Tbsp cookies or 6 ⅓-cup cookies.

Sunflower Chocolate or Carob Spirulina Brownies

4 Cups Raw Hulled Sunflower Seeds
½ Cup Water
⅓ Cup Honey, Agave Nectar, or Coconut Palm Syrup
1 tsp Vanilla Extract, or Seeds from ½ of a Vanilla Bean Pod
½ Cup Raw Carob Powder or Raw Cacao
1 Tbsp Spirulina

Soak the sunflower seeds for at least 7 hours, then strain and rinse well. Preheat your dehydrator to 115°. Place the seeds and water into the food processor. Process until the sunflower seeds have become a pâté. Add the remaining ingredients and combine thoroughly. Scoop and shape into ⅓ cup or 1 Tbsp cookies on parchment paper. Dehydrate for 22 hours at 115°.

Sprouted Sunflower Carob Coconut Brownies

4 Cups Raw Hulled Sunflower Seeds
½ Cup Water
⅓ Cup Honey
1 tsp Vanilla Extract, or Seeds from ½ of a Vanilla Bean Pod
½ Cup Raw Carob Powder
⅓ + ⅓ Cup Shredded Coconut

Soak the sunflower seeds for a minimum of 7 hours, then strain and thoroughly rinse them. Preheat your dehydrator to 115°. Place the seeds and ⅓ cup water into the food processor. Process until the sunflower seeds have become a pâté. Add the remaining ingredients (except for the second ⅓ cup of coconut), and mix thoroughly. Scoop and shape into ⅓ cup or 1 Tbsp cookies on a dehydrator tray lined with parchment paper. Sprinkle the remaining ⅓ cup of shredded coconut over the top of your cookies. Dehydrate for about 22 hours at 115°.

Sprouted Sunflower Apricot Almond Blondies

4 Cups Raw Hulled Sunflower Seeds
½ Cup Water
1 tsp Vanilla Extract, or Seeds from ½ of a Vanilla Bean Pod
⅓ Cup Raw Honey, Agave Nectar, or Coconut Palm Syrup
1 Tbsp Cinnamon
½ Cup Raw Almonds
1 Cup Dried Turkish Apricots (Diced)

Soak the sunflower seeds and almonds *separately* for a minimum of 7 hours. Once the soak is complete, *separately* strain and rinse both well. Preheat your dehydrator to 115°. Place the sunflower seeds and ½ cup water into the food processor. Process until the sunflower seeds have become a pâté. Transfer the pâté to a large mixing bowl. Add the sweetener, vanilla, and cinnamon, and mix. Next, add the sprouted almonds (saving a few to decorate your cookies) and the chopped apricots.

Now, you are ready to scoop and shape ⅓ cup or 1 Tbsp cookies on a dehydrator tray lined with parchment paper. Place an almond or two on your cookies before dehydrating. Dehydrate for approximately 22 hours at 115°.

❖

Lite 'N Seedy Sweet Breads (No soaking required)

The following breads are full of flavor and are lower in carbohydrates than the previous nut breads. The base of these Lite 'N Seedy Sweet Breads is fruit, rather than grains and nuts. **These breads do not require soaking.** So, if you were not able to get a soak going the night before, but you are ready to make some bread, the following recipes are a great option! Also, these breads are a fabulous way to preserve the harvest. When you or your local farmer has an abundance of zucchini, apples, or bananas, make many of these loaves of bread, and put them in the freezer.

Apple Lavender Date Lite 'n Seedy Bread

4 Large Apples
2-3 Cups Fresh Ground Flax Seeds
⅓ Cup Honey, Agave Nectar, or Coconut Palm Syrup
1 tsp Sea Salt
1 Tbsp Lavender   **Yields 5 Large Loaves**
1 Cup Pitted and Diced Dates   **or 15 Cookies**

Preheat your dehydrator to 115°. Core the apples and place them into the food processor or blender. Purée them well. Add the lavender to this mix and process for about one minute. Transfer this apple-lavender purée into a large mixing bowl. Add the flax seeds (between 2 and 3 cups, adding enough to bind the dough), sweetener, and sea salt. Finally, fold in the pitted and finely-diced dates.

Using measuring cups, create 1 cup-sized loaves or ⅓ cup-sized cookies on your dehydrator tray lined with parchment paper. Place some thin slices of apple, a little sprig of lavender, or sprinkle some lavender on the top of the cookies or loaves for extra appeal. The loaves will dehydrate at 115° for 26 hours and the cookies at 115° for 22 hours. They smell great!

Apple Cinnamon Spice Lite 'n Seedy Bread

4 Large Apples
2-3 Cups Fresh Ground Flax Seeds
⅓ Cup Honey, Agave Nectar, or Coconut Palm Syrup
1 tsp Sea Salt   **Yields 5 Large Loaves**
1 Tbsp Cinnamon   **or 15 Cookies**

Preheat your dehydrator to 115°. Core the apples, place them into the food processor or blender, and purée. Transfer this apple purée into a large mixing bowl. Add the flax seeds (between 2 and 3 cups, adding enough to bind the dough), cinnamon, sea salt, and sweetener.

Use measuring cups to create 1 cup-sized loaves, or ⅓ cup-sized cookies. Adorn with a thin slice of apple. The loaves will dehydrate at 115° for 26 hours, and the cookies dehydrate at 115° for 22 hours.

Banana Lite 'n Seedy Bread

4 Cups Chopped Bananas
2-3 Cups Fresh Ground Flax Seeds   **Yields 3 Large Loaves**
1 tsp Sea Salt   **or 8 Cookies**

Preheat your dehydrator to 115°. Place bananas in your food processor and process them into a mash. Transfer to a large mixing bowl. Add the fresh ground flax seeds (between 1 and 2 cups, adding enough to bind the dough) and sea salt.

You can shape this into 1 cup loaves or ⅓ cup cookies, or you can spread 3 cups of this sweet dough onto your dehydrator trays fitted with unbleached parchment paper. Spread evenly until the bread is about ½ inch thick, and then score to create square slices of bread. Very convenient as a morning toast or for scooping a sweet spread (see page 125 for an example)!

In a café, there are options for every aspect of your being. Do you need a warm, rich soup or drink? Do you need something sweet, or something savory? Do you need something cool and crisp? This recipe book is the live creative café of your dreams. This is the art of à la carte. Have all the elements of your taste centers available to you.

These savory breads are a lovely foundational food. Full of good fats, proteins, and flavor, they not only delight, they satiate. Delight and savor their piquant flavors and feel their deep nutrition.

Garlic Rosemary Sprouted Live Bread

1 Cup Raw Brazil Nuts, Pecans or Walnuts
1 Cup Raw Buckwheat Groats or Other Raw Grains
1-2 Cups Fresh Ground Flax Seeds
½ Cup Water
⅓ Cup Olive Oil
2 Fresh Garlic Cloves or 1 Tbsp Garlic Powder
1 tsp Sea Salt   **Yields 4-5 Large Loaves**
2 Tbsp Rosemary   **or 15 Biscuits**

Soak buckwheat and nuts for at least 7 hours. Once the grains and nuts have soaked, place them into a colander or a sieve and rinse well. Preheat your dehydrator to 115°. Transfer the grains and nuts to the food processor. While the processor is running, add ½ cup of water. Once the grains and nuts are well combined, add the olive oil, freshly ground flax seeds, sea salt, garlic, and rosemary. Add the flax until you get a nice shapeable consistency.

Use measuring cups to create uniform sized loaves. Scoop 1 cup of the bread dough, place it on your dehydrator tray lined with parchment paper, and shape into an attractive loaf. Repeat. Or, use your ⅓ cup measurer to scoop the dough and shape into convenient biscuits. Adorn these breads and biscuits with rosemary—very attractive! The loaves will dehydrate at 115° for 26 hours, and the biscuits at 115° for 22 hours. Freeze or store in the refrigerator.

You can also make a personal pizza! Place 1 cup of the dough on your parchment paper, and spread into a circle. Pre-score your slices with a knife. Depending on thickness, the crust will be done in about 4 hours. A personal pizza can be topped with a savory spread (see pages 70-75), grated fresh veggies, and a drizzle of cashew cream (page 78). Fantastic!

Kalamata Olive Herb Sprouted Live Bread

1 Cup Raw Walnuts, Brazil Nuts or Pecans
1 Cup Raw Buckwheat Groats or Other Raw Grains
1-2 Cups Fresh Ground Flax Seeds
⅓ Cup Olive Oil
½ Cup Water
1 Fresh Garlic Clove or 1 tsp Garlic Powder
1 ½ tsp Sea Salt   **Yields 4-5 Large Loaves**
2 Tbsp Italian Herbs   **or 15 Biscuits**
⅓ + ⅓ Cup Kalamata Olives (Pitted and Sliced)

Soak buckwheat and nuts for at least 7 hours. Once the grains and nuts have soaked, place them in a colander, making sure the holes are small enough that you don't lose a lot of grain, and rinse well. Preheat your dehydrator to 115°. Move the grains and nuts to the food processor, being sure not to overfill. While the processor is running, add ½ cup of water. Once the grains and nuts are well combined, add the olive oil, freshly ground flax seeds, sea salt, garlic, and Italian herbs. Once this is thoroughly processed, fold in ⅓ cup Kalamata olives. Save the remaining ⅓ cup for placing on top of the biscuits or loaves just before they go into the dehydrator.

Now, create 1 cup-sized loaves or ⅓ cup biscuits on your dehydrator tray lined with unbleached parchment. Place a few olives and/or sprinkle some herbs on top of the loaves or biscuits for an attractive finish. The loaves will dehydrate at 115° for 26 hours and the biscuits at 115° for 22 hours. Freeze or store in the refrigerator what you cannot use in a week.

Also, try making a personal pizza by measuring 1 cup and spreading to the desired thickness, and pre-score your slices. Top this with a savory spread (pages 70-75), grated fresh veggies, and a drizzle of cashew cream (page 78).

Sprouted Live Pesto Savory Rolls & Calzones

1 Cup Raw Walnuts, Brazil Nuts, or Pecans
1 Cup Raw Buckwheat Groats or other Raw Grains
1-2 Cups Fresh Ground Flax Seeds
⅓ Cup Olive Oil
½ Cup Water
2 Fresh Garlic Cloves, or 1 Tbsp Garlic Powder
1 ½ tsp Sea Salt
2 Tbsp Italian Herbs   **Yields 4-5 Savory Rolls**

Creamy Basil Pesto:
6 Ounces of Fresh Basil (Cleaned & Dried)
2-3 Garlic Cloves
3 Tbsp Lemon Juice
2 tsp Sea Salt
1 Cup Soaked Cashews, Macadamia Nuts, or Walnuts
½ Cup Olive Oil

Soak the buckwheat and nuts for a minimum of 7 hours.

When the soak is complete, rinse them well. Preheat your dehydrator to 115°. Transfer the grains and nuts to the food processor. While the processor is running, add ½ cup of water. Once the grains and nuts are well combined, add the olive oil, freshly ground flax seeds, sea salt, garlic, and Italian herbs. Mix well and set aside.

To make the Creamy Basil Pesto, place the fresh basil in the food processor along with the garlic, lemon juice, and sea salt. Once the basil is thoroughly chopped, add the cashews, macadamia nuts, or walnuts, and the olive oil. Purée all of these ingredients until you have a fabulous pesto.

To make these savory rolls, place 2 cups of dough onto your unbleached parchment paper and spread it out. The goal is a square that measures approximately 10" X 10". The dough needs to be spread very evenly to about ⅓ inch thick.

Now, spread the pesto in a nice thick, creamy strip down one of the sides, close to the edge, about 2" wide. This is where we will begin to roll. Using the parchment paper as you would a sushi rolling mat, lift this edge of the dough and begin to roll it over. Allow the parchment to separate from the roll once the bread is rolling onto itself. You can use your hands to further smooth and shape this large roll. Finally, cut the savory roll into 3 inch sections to be dehydrated.

You may also choose make calzones instead of rolls. To do this, place 1 cup dough balls onto your unbleached parchment paper. Using damp hands, shape each ball into a small loaf. With your fingers, depress the center of this loaf and create a basin. Into this basin, place as much pesto as it can hold, then close the basin around the pesto. It looks great if a little pesto is peeking out from the center, so don't worry about getting it completely closed.

These rolls and calzones can be garnished with pine nuts or chopped macadamia nuts. Dehydrate at 115° for about 24 hours.

Freeze breads that you will not use in the next week and store the rest in the refrigerator in an air-tight container.

Sprouted Live Sun-Dried Tomato Rolls & Calzones

1 Cup Raw Walnuts, Brazil Nuts or Pecans
1 Cup Raw Buckwheat Groats or Other Raw Grains
1-2 Cups Fresh Ground Flax Seeds
⅓ Cup Olive Oil
½ Cup Water
1 Large Garlic Clove or 1 tsp Garlic Powder
1 tsp Sea Salt
2 Tbsp Italian Herbs   **Yields 4-5 Savory Rolls**

Sun-Dried Tomato Pesto
1 Cup tightly packed Sun-Dried Tomatoes (Dry or packed in olive oil; if using dry, soak first for at least 20 min.)
2 Large Garlic Cloves
1 Tbsp Lemon Juice
1 ½ tsp Honey
½ tsp Sea Salt
½ tsp Red Pepper Flakes (Optional, for a little spice)
½ Cup Walnuts, Macadamia Nuts or Pine Nuts
¼ Cup Olive Oil (Suggestion: If you are using tomatoes packed in olive oil, include that oil in this measurement)

Soak buckwheat and nuts for a minimum of 7 hours.

When the soak is complete, place them in a colander, making sure the holes are small enough that you don't lose too much grain, and rinse well. Preheat your dehydrator to 115°. Now, move these grains and nuts to the food processor. While the processor is running, add ½ cup of water. Once the grains and nuts are well combined, add the olive oil, freshly ground flax seeds, sea salt, garlic, and Italian herbs. Blend well and set aside.

To make the Sun-Dried Tomato Pesto, place all of the ingredients into the food processor and blend until smooth. You may need to support the processor while the tomatoes are being chopped.

Use the same method described in the previous recipe to make the savory pesto rolls. Place 2 cups of dough onto your unbleached parchment paper and spread it out. The goal is a square that measures approximately 10" X 10". The dough needs to be spread very evenly, to about ⅓ inch thick. Using your spatula and hands, shape the savory dough.

Next, spread the pesto in a nice thick, creamy strip down one of the sides, close to the edge, about 2" wide. This is where we will begin our roll. Using the parchment paper, as you would a sushi rolling mat, lift this edge of the dough and begin to roll it over. Allow the parchment to separate from the roll once the bread is rolling onto itself. You can use your hands to further smooth and shape this large roll. Next, cut the savory roll into 3 inch sections to be dehydrated.

You could also make calzones. Place 1 cup of dough onto your parchment. Using damp hands, shape the dough into a small loaf. With your fingers, depress the center of this loaf and create a basin. Into this basin, insert as much pesto as it can hold, and then close the basin around the pesto. It looks great if a little pesto is peeking out from the center, so don't worry about getting it completely closed. Repeat this to make more calzones.

Dehydrate the rolls and calzones at 115° for 24 hours.

Freeze breads that you will not use in the next week and store the rest in the refrigerator in an air-tight container.

Lite 'N Seedy Savory Breads & Tortillas

The following highly flavorful and nutritious savory breads are comprised of seeds and vegetables, without nuts or grains. They are lower in carbs and less heavy. Making these breads is an excellent way to preserve an abundant harvest. They are a cornerstone food in our kitchen!

Live Sweet Onion Bread, Biscuit & Tortillas

4 Large Sweet Onions (Peeled & Chopped)
2 Cups Fresh Ground Sunflower Seeds
2 Cups Fresh Ground Flax Seeds
2 Tbsp Honey or Agave Nectar   **Yields 4-5 Large Loaves**
1 Tbsp Tamari   **or 15 Biscuits**

Chopping onions will likely have a strong impact on your tear ducts. To lessen, refrigerate them in advance, open windows, and warn anybody in the house.

Preheat your dehydrator to 115°. Place the onions into the food processor and purée them. Pour the onions into a large mixing bowl. Add the remaining ingredients and mix well. Create 1 cup sized loaves or ⅓ cup biscuits. Place the dough on your dehydrator tray fitted with parchment paper, and shape. The loaves will dehydrate at 115° for 26 hours, and the biscuits at 115° for 22 hours.

You can also make tortillas. Place ⅓ cup of dough on the parchment and spread it out very, very thin: about one-eighth of an inch. Dehydrate these for 3-4 hours. Fill it with sprouts n' spreads and roll it into a wrap. How about a pizza? Spread the dough to the desired thickness, score your slices, and dry for about 4 hours. Top with spreads (pages 70-75) and veggies.

Live Sun-Dried Tomato Onion Bread & Tortillas

4 Large Sweet Onions (Peeled & Chopped)
2 Cups Fresh Ground Sunflower Seeds
2 Cups Fresh Ground Flax Seeds
1 Cup Sun Dried Tomatoes (Dry or Packed in Olive Oil)
2 Tbsp Honey or Agave Nectar
1 Tbsp Tamari   **Yields 4-5 Large Loaves**
1-2 Tbsp of Italian Herbs   **or 15 Biscuits**

If you are using *dry* sun-dried tomatoes, soak them in warm water for at least 20 minutes. You do not need to soak tomatoes packed in oil.

Create good ventilation for chopping onions; refrigerated onions are less tearful. Preheat your dehydrator to 115°. Next, place the chopped onions and sun-dried tomatoes into the food processor. Pulse them, then purée them. Note: Support your food processor with strong hands and arms because the dried tomatoes can give the appliance quite a jolt before they begin to blend. Pour the onion and tomato purée into a large mixing bowl. Add the remaining ingredients and mix well.

Create 1 cup loaves or ⅓ cup biscuits from the bread dough on unbleached parchment on your dehydrator tray. At this point, you can sprinkle the Italian herbs over the top of the biscuits and/or loaves. The loaves will dehydrate at 115° for 26 hours and the biscuits at 115° for 22 hours.

Alternatively, you can make tortillas. Spread out ⅓ cups of dough to one-eighth inch thick on your parchment paper and dehydrate them for 3-4 hours. They will come out soft and ready to roll up into a great lunch! This dough can also be dried as a pizza crust!

Freeze any breads or tortillas that you will not use in the next week and store the rest in the refrigerator in an air-tight container.

The Chips and Crackers in this section are so filled with flavor, I dare say most conventional crackers and chips taste like cardboard in comparison.

They are great for preserving the harvest, since they do not require refrigeration or freezing. The crackers will store for many months in an airtight container. They keep their crunch, their flavor, and their fantastic nutrition ready for you!

C·R·A·C·K·E·R·S

Jeff Eichler ©2012

Live Sweet Onion Crackers

4 Large Sweet Onions (Peeled & Chopped)
2 Cups Fresh Ground Flax Seeds
2 Cups Fresh Ground Sunflower Seeds
1 Tbsp Honey or Agave Nectar
1 Tbsp Tamari   **Yields 2 Trays of Crackers**

Note: The onions in this recipe can send people crying, not to mention the chef. So be ready: clear out the house, open a window, turn on the fan, and wear goggles if you need to! Refrigerated onions create *fewer* tears.

Preheat your dehydrator to 115°. Place the onions into the food processor and pulse them down into a purée. Transfer this onion purée into a large mixing bowl. Add the remaining ingredients and stir well with a mixing spoon.

You are now ready to spread this savory dough onto your dehydrator tray lined with unbleached parchment paper. Using a spatula, paint a very thin layer of dough across the entire tray, approximately one-eighth inch thick. Once the mixture is uniformly spread, score the crackers by using the edge of your spatula or butter knife to draw a straight line down the entire tray, dividing it in half. Then, repeat to divide further. Next, draw perpendicular lines, forming a checkered pattern. Repeat this scoring until you have made crackers of the desired size. When the crackers are dry, you can easily break them along these scores.

Place your crackers in the dehydrator at 115° for 26 hours. Break up the crackers and enjoy! These crackers store well in your pantry and will keep for many months.

What a wonderful way to preserve a great onion harvest!

Live Corn Cilantro Tortilla Chips and Tortillas

4 Cups Frozen or Fresh Corn
1 Large Bunch of Cilantro (Remove thick, woody stems)
½ Cup Water
2 Cups Fresh Ground Flax Seeds
1 tsp Sea Salt
½ tsp Turmeric   **Yields 1 Tray of Crackers**
1 Tbsp Chili Powder (Optional)

Thaw the corn if necessary. Preheat your dehydrator to 115°.
Purée the corn kernels along with ½ cup water in the food
processor using the S-blade. Add the cilantro to this purée and
blend until very well combined. Pour this purée into a large
mixing bowl. Add the remaining ingredients and mix well.
Adding the optional chili powder will provide a spicy kick!

Transfer this mixture to your dehydrator tray, with unbleached
parchment in place. Use a spatula to paint an approximately
one-eighth inch thick layer, uniformly covering the entire tray.
Once the mixture is spread, score the crackers. To do this, take
the edge of your spatula or knife and draw a straight line down
the entire tray and repeat. Then draw perpendicular lines that
form a checker-board pattern. You can make the crackers
large or small. You can even shape them into triangles, like
traditional tortilla chips.

Place your crackers in the dehydrator at 115° for 26 hours.
Break them up and enjoy! These crackers store great in your
pantry and will keep for many months.

To make the most delicious corn tortillas, measure ⅓ cup of the
corn dough onto your parchment covered dehydrator tray and
spread very thin—one-eighth inch works great. Allow these
nutritious little circles to dehydrate for 3-4 hours.

Live Garlic Corn Chips and Tortillas

4 Cups Frozen or Fresh Corn Kernels
½ Cup Water
2 Large Garlic Cloves
2 Cups Fresh Ground Flax Seeds
½ tsp Turmeric (Optional)
1 tsp Sea Salt   **Yields 1 Tray of Crackers**

Preheat your dehydrator to 115°. Thaw and purée the corn kernels with ½ cup of water and garlic in the food processor or blender. Pour this purée into a large mixing bowl, add the remaining ingredients, and combine.

Transfer this mixture to your dehydrator tray, with unbleached parchment in place. Using a spatula, paint an approximately one-eighth inch thick layer, uniformly covering the entire tray. Once the mixture is uniformly spread, score the crackers using the edge of your spatula.

Place your crackers in the dehydrator at 115° for 26 hours. Break up the crackers and enjoy! These crackers store great in your pantry and will keep for many months.

To make delicious Garlic Corn Tortillas, measure ⅓ cup of the garlic corn tortilla dough onto your parchment covered dehydrator tray, and spread very thin: one-eighth inch works great. Allow these nutritious little circles to dehydrate for 3-4 hours.

Live Basil Pesto Cashew Crackers

6 Ounces of Fresh Basil
2 Large Garlic Cloves
3 Tbsp Lemon Juice
2 tsp Sea Salt
3 Cups Cashews (Soaked for 2 Hours, Drained & Rinsed)
½ Cup Olive Oil
½-1 Cup Water   **Yields 2 Trays of Crackers**
2 Cups Fresh Ground Flax Seeds

Preheat your dehydrator to 115°. Place the fresh basil in the food processor or blender, and add garlic, lemon juice, and sea salt. Blend these ingredients until you have a nice purée. Next, add the soaked cashews and olive oil. While the cashews are blending, add the water. You can substitute macadamia nuts, which are delicious, more nutritious, and do not need a soak.

Pour this completely delicious purée into a large mixing bowl. Add the flax seeds and stir well. Transfer this mixture to your dehydrator tray lined with unbleached parchment. Use a spatula to paint a thin layer approximately one-eighth inch thick that covers the entire tray. Once the mixture is uniformly spread, score the crackers by taking the edge of your spatula and drawing straight lines down and across the entire tray, forming a checkered pattern. You can choose to make large crackers or small this way. When the crackers are dry, you can easily break them along these scores.

Place your crackers in the dehydrator at 115° for 26 hours. Break them up and enjoy!

This recipe also makes for a wonderful pizza crust. Spread the dough out in the desired shape, about ¼" thick and dry for approximately 4 hours.

This is another great way to preserve that fantastic basil harvest and support your local farmers!

Live Red Pepper Cashew Crackers

3 Large Sweet Red Peppers (Cored & Chopped)
2-3 Large Garlic Cloves
¼ Cup Olive Oil
2 Tbsp Lemon Juice
1 Tbsp Sea Salt
3 Cups Cashews (Soaked for 2 Hours, Drained & Rinsed)
½ Cup Water   **Yields 2 Trays of Crackers**
2 Cups Fresh Ground Flax Seeds

Preheat your dehydrator to 115°. Place the fresh peppers in the food processor and add the garlic, lemon juice, olive oil, and sea salt. Combine these ingredients into a fabulous pesto. Pour the soaked cashews into a colander and rinse well. Add these cashews to the pesto. While the cashews are blending, add water. You can also substitute macadamia nuts, which are delicious, more nutritious, and do not need a soak.

Pour this fabulous purée into a large mixing bowl. Add the fresh-ground flax seeds and stir well. Now transfer this mixture to your dehydrator tray lined with unbleached parchment paper. Using a spatula, paint an approximately one-eighth inch thick layer that covers the entire tray. Once the mixture is uniformly spread, score the crackers using the edge of your spatula.

Place your crackers in the dehydrator at 115° for 26 hours. Break up the crackers and enjoy! These crackers store great in your pantry and will keep for many months.

This recipe also makes for a wonderful pizza crust. Just spread the dough out in the desired shape, about ¼ inch thick, and dry for approximately 4 hours.

Live Nut Toast

3 Cups Nut Pulp (From making Nut Milks)
1 ½ Cup Fresh Ground Flax Seeds
½ Cup Whole Flax Seed
1 Cup Water
1 Tbsp Caraway and/or Coriander Seeds
1 tsp Sea Salt   **Yields 2 Trays of Crackers**

This is a simple recipe but it is so, so good. Preheat your dehydrator to 115°. Combine all elements in a mixing bowl and spread about ¼ inch thick on your dehydrator tray lined with unbleached parchment. Score into large squares with the edge of a spatula. Dry at 115° for 24 hours. Enjoy!

Live Zucchini Crackers and Tortillas

2 Cups Chopped Zucchini
1 Cup Fresh Ground Flax Seed
¼ Cup Whole Flax Seed
½ Cup Soaked Pecans or Walnuts (Soak for 7+ hours)
1 Tbsp Lemon Juice
½ tsp Sea Salt   **Yields 2 Trays of Crackers**

Place the zucchini and soaked nuts into the food processor. Pulse these ingredients into a course purée. Pour into a large mixing bowl and add the remaining ingredients. Stir to combine. Next, transfer this mixture to your dehydrator trays (lined with unbleached parchment paper) and paint a thin layer, taking care that it is evenly spread with no holes, thin spots, or thick spots. Score the crackers into the desired shape and size. When the crackers are dry, you can easily break along these lines. Dry at 115° for 26 hours.

To make tortillas, measure ⅓ cup of the dough onto your parchment covered dehydrator tray, and spread very thin: one-eighth inch works great. Allow to dehydrate for 3-4 hours.

Kale Chips—What fun! Add fresh Calendula flower petals to your Kale Chip Recipes *after* you have coated them with dressing. Beautiful and Healthy, just like you…

Kale Chips

1 Large Bunch of Curly Kale (Purple and/or Green)
¼ Cup Organic Raw Tahini
¼ Cup Sunflower Seeds
1 tsp Sea Salt
1 tsp Turmeric Powder
¼ Cup Water
¼ Cup Nutritional Yeast (Large Flakes Work Best)

Wash your kale thoroughly. De-stem the leaves. Place the leafy part of the greens in a large mixing bowl. Place the dry ingredients: sunflower seeds, sea salt, turmeric and nutritional yeast into your food processor. Process into a fine flour. Now add the tahini and water to make a creamy dressing. Pour this mix over your greens and massage the leaves. Really rub the dressings in. Spread the coated leaves onto your dehydrator trays (with or without parchment paper) and dehydrate at 115° overnight, or for about 15 hours.

Curry Kale Chips

1 Large Bunch of Curly Kale
¼ Cup Organic Raw Tahini
¼ Cup Sunflower Seeds
1 tsp Sea Salt
⅓ Cup Water
¼ Cup Nutritional Yeast
1 ½ Tbsp Curry Powder

Follow the instructions on the above recipe, adding the curry powder for some amazing flavor and warmth. A real crowd pleaser!

Cashew Red Pepper Kale Chips

1 Large Bunch of Curly Kale
1 Cup Cashews (Soak for 2 Hours, then Rinse & Drain)
⅓ Cup Water
1 Sweet Red Pepper
1-2 Garlic Cloves
1 tsp Sea Salt
1 Tbsp Lemon Juice
1 tsp Italian Herbs
1 Tbsp Nutritional Yeast (Optional)

Place the soaked cashews and water into the food processor or blender, and blend them into a slurry. Add the remaining ingredients except the kale. This is your dressing. Now, wash the kale thoroughly and de-stem. Place the leafy part of the kale into a large mixing bowl. Once you've done the entire bunch, pour the Cashew Red Pepper Dressing over the kale. With strong hands, really rub the dressings into the kale. Once all of the leaves have been massaged and thoroughly coated, place them in the dehydrator at 115° for 15 hours.

Sweet Dreamsicle Kale Chips (a.k.a. "Kale Candy")

1 Large Bunch of Curly Kale
1 Cup Soaked Pumpkin Seeds
2 Pitted Dates
⅓ Cup Agave Nectar, Honey, or Coconut Palm Syrup
½ Medium Orange, with Seeds Removed & Rind On
¼ Cup Water
1 Tbsp Spirulina
1 tsp Vanilla Extract, or Seeds from ½ of a Vanilla Bean Pod
Pinch Sea Salt

Follow the method of previous recipes: processing kale and blending the remaining ingredients to make the dressing. Thoroughly coat leaves and dehydrate at 115° until dry.

Take a moment to consider that a sprouted grain, nut or seed carries the potential to grow an entire plant or tree.

Know that in the germination process, the nutrients made available to your body are multiplied many times over.

Sprouted Live Granola makes a wonderful meal in the morning and an excellent trail mix for energy on the go.
Enjoy!

RAWNOLA

Jeff Eichen

Coconut Almond Sprouted Live Granola

2 Cups Raw Buckwheat Groats
1 Cup Raw Almonds
1 Cup Raw Pumpkin Seeds
1 Cup Raw Sunflower Seeds
2 Cups Cored & Shredded Apples (About 4 Apples)
2 Bananas
½ Cup Pitted Dates, Coconut Dates, or Date Paste
½ Cup Shredded Coconut
¼ Cup Water
1 Tbsp Cinnamon
1 Tbsp Nutmeg
1 tsp Sea Salt

Soak the buckwheat, almonds, pumpkin, and sunflower seeds overnight, or for a minimum of 7 hours. Pour into a colander and rinse well, taking care that the holes in the colander are small enough that you do not lose much buckwheat. Preheat your dehydrator to 115°. Transfer the mix to your mixing bowl. Clean, core, and shred your apples, either manually or with a food processor. Add the shredded apple and shredded coconut to the buckwheat. Place the remaining ingredients in the food processor or blender and blend well. Pour this over the grains and apples, and mix, folding the ingredients together. Now, lay the Sprouted Live Granola out on your dehydrator trays and dehydrate for at least 26 hours at 115°.

This fantastic breakfast food keeps for months in a sealed bag, plastic container, or glass jar.

See the chapter on Fresh Nut & Seed Milks (page 92) for great live milk recipes to enhance your Sprouted Live Granola creation. Or just eat as a lovely sprouted snack.

For a warm, soft breakfast cereal, pour warm water over your Rawnola and let it soak for 10 minutes before eating.

Cranberry Hazelnut Sprouted Live Granola

2 Cups Raw Buckwheat Groats
1 Cup Raw Hazelnuts
½ Cup Raw Pumpkin Seeds
½ Cup Raw Sunflower Seeds
2 Cups Cored & Shredded Apples (About 4 Apples)
½ Cup Pitted Dates, Coco Dates, or Date Paste
¼ Cup Water
1 Tbsp Cinnamon
1 Tbsp Nutmeg
1 tsp Sea Salt
2 Cups Juice Sweetened Dried Cranberries

Soak buckwheat, hazelnuts, pumpkin seeds, and sunflower seeds overnight, or for a minimum of 7 hours. Pour them into a colander and rinse well, making sure the holes of the colander are small enough to keep the buckwheat in. Preheat your dehydrator to 115°. Transfer them to your mixing bowl. Clean, core, and shred your apples, either manually or with a food processor. Mix the shredded apples, hazelnuts, seeds, and buckwheat. Place the remaining ingredients (except for the cranberries) into the food processor or blender and blend well. Pour this mix over the grains and apples, and mix. Now, lay the Sprouted Live Granola out on your dehydrator trays lined with unbleached parchment paper, and dehydrate for at least 26 hours at 115°.

After you take the Sprouted Live Granola out of the dehydrator, add the dried cranberries.

This fabulous breakfast food keeps for months in a sealed bag, plastic container, or glass jar.

For a warm, soft breakfast cereal, pour warm water over your Rawnola and let it soak for 10 minutes before eating.

Maple Pecan Sprouted Live Granola

2 Cups Raw Buckwheat Groats
1 Cup Raw Pecans
½ Cup Raw Pumpkin Seeds
½ Cup Raw Sunflower Seeds
2 Cups Cored & Shredded Apples (About 4 Medium Apples)
½ Cup Maple Syrup
½ Cups Pitted Dates, Coconut Dates, or Date Paste
¼ Cup Water
1 Tbsp Cinnamon
1 tsp Sea Salt

Soak the buckwheat, pecans, pumpkin seeds, and sunflower seeds overnight, or for a minimum of 7 hours. Pour them into a colander and rinse well. Preheat your dehydrator to 115°. Transfer them to your mixing bowl. Clean, core, and shred the apples, either manually or with a food processor. Mix the shredded apples, pecans, seeds and buckwheat. Place the remaining ingredients in the blender, and blend well. Pour this sweet dressing over the grains, nuts, and apples, and mix. Finally, lay the Sprouted Live Granola out on your dehydrator trays, lined with unbleached parchment paper, and dehydrate for 26 hours at 115°.

This amazing breakfast food keeps for months, sealed airtight.

To enjoy it as a warm cereal, pour warm water over your Rawnola, and let it soak for 10 minutes before eating.

Valencia Fig Sprouted Live Granola

2 Cups Raw Buckwheat Groats
1 Cup Raw Brazil Nuts, Coarsely Chopped
½ Cup Raw Pumpkin Seeds
½ Cup Raw Sunflower Seeds
2 Cups Cored & Shredded Apples (About 4 Medium Apples)
¼ Cup Honey
2 Medium Oranges (With rind, but *without* the bitter seeds!)
1 Tbsp Cinnamon
1 tsp Sea Salt
1 -2 Cups Chopped Dried Figs (Calimyrna or Black Mission)

Soak the chopped Brazil nuts, buckwheat, pumpkin seeds, and sunflower seeds overnight, or for minimum of 7 hours. Once the soak is complete, pour the buckwheat, nuts, and seeds into a colander and rinse well. Preheat your dehydrator to 115°. Transfer them to your mixing bowl. Clean, core, and shred the apples, either manually or with a food processor. Mix the shredded apples, chopped Brazil nuts, seeds, and buckwheat. Place the remaining ingredients, with the exception of the figs, in the blender, and blend well. Pour this mix over the grains and apples, and combine well. Now lay the sprouted live cereal out on your dehydrator trays, lined with unbleached parchment paper, and dehydrate for at least 26 hours at 115°. Once the cereal is thoroughly dried, add the chopped and dried figs.

This sensational breakfast food keeps for months, sealed airtight.

For a warm, soft breakfast cereal, pour warm water over the Rawnola, and let it soak for 10 minutes before eating. Delicious!

A Salad is a play of textures, tastes and colors.

There is the stage:
It may be sprouted lentils, romaine lettuce, or spiralized sweet potato.

To this is added the soundtrack:
The dressing, with its richness, tanginess, saltiness, and herbalness.

Over the top are the actors:
Crunch, zest, and juiciness.

Bravo!

SALADS

Jeff Eichman © 2012

Sprouts...

There are many ways to sprout seeds and beans. I have found huge success with sprouting using a simple method. I prefer this method because it is easier to sprout large batches and the sprouts stay fresh longer. I still use sprouting jars and bags for tiny sprouts like mustard, clover, and alfalfa. When I am sprouting adzuki, mung, lentil, or garbanzo beans, or sunflower seeds, here is how I do it:

Soak the beans or seeds for 24 hours in a large bowl completely submerged in pure water. When 24 hours have gone by, I pour the soaked beans or seeds into a colander and rinse very, very well. I let the beans or seeds stay in that colander for at least another day, but sometimes up to 3 days. I place the colander directly into the sink to make rinsing them often and thoroughly very easy. If I need to use my sink and need to move the sprouts, I put the entire colander into a large mixing bowl, or on a plate. When the sink is available again, I transfer the colander back to the sink. I rinse the sprouts every few hours, but no less than 2-3 times per day. Being rinsed often in the colander keeps air and water readily available to the germinating sprouts.

The results are fresh, crunchy, and delicious. Once they have really begun to grow, at day two or three, I transfer them into a container and into the fridge. I find sprouts keep for about a week, depending on the variety. I always give them a thorough rinse before making a salad or a hummus with them.

Sprouted Mung Bean & Arame Ocean Salad

3 Cups Sprouted Mung Beans
1 Cup Dry Arame Seaweed
3 Tbsp Brown Rice Vinegar
2 Tbsp Tamari
1 Tbsp Sesame Oil
2 Tbsp Honey
2 Crushed Garlic Cloves or 1 tsp Garlic Powder
½ Medium Cucumber
3 Diced Green Onions
1 Tbsp Red Pepper Flakes
2 Tbsp Sesame Seeds   **Serves 3-4**

Soak the seaweed for 20 minutes, then strain. Mix the rehydrated seaweed with the mung bean sprouts. Separately, whisk or blend all of the remaining ingredients. Toss everything together and enjoy!

Simple Caesar Lentil Salad

3 Cups Sprouted Green Lentils
2 Tbsp Olive Oil
2 Tbsp Lemon Juice
½ tsp Sea Salt
2 Garlic Cloves or ½ tsp Garlic Powder
1 Tbsp of Nutritional Yeast (Optional)
Fresh Ground Black Pepper (To taste)   **Serves 3-4**

Place the olive oil, lemon juice, sea salt, garlic, and optional yeast into a blender and combine very well. Pour this dressing over your sprouted lentils and toss. Add other fresh veggies (i.e. shredded purple cabbage, diced red pepper, tomatoes, dill, chopped dark leafy greens, red onion, etc.) for more fun and color. Enjoy and store remainder in the refrigerator to have for lunch the next day.

Sprouted Lentil Salad with Shiitake Dressing

4 Cups Sprouted Green Lentils
¼ Cup Olive Oil
1 ½ Tbsp Apple Cider Vinegar
2 Tbsp Tamari
1 Tbsp Sesame Oil
1 tsp Honey or Agave Nectar
1 Tbsp Sesame Seeds
½ Cup Chopped Shiitake Mushrooms
1 Cup Grape or Cherry Tomatoes (Sliced in Half)
1 Tbsp Red Pepper Flakes (Optional)   **Serves 3-4**

First, place the olive oil, vinegar, tamari, sesame oil, sesame seeds, and honey into the blender. Blend these ingredients for about 30 seconds, then add the mushrooms. Pour the dressing into your lentils and toss the tomatoes and dressing.

Shredded Beet Carrot Walnut Salad

2 Peeled Medium Beets
4 Peeled Large Carrots
¼ Cup Olive Oil
2 Tbsp Honey
¼ Cup Pure Water
½ tsp Sea Salt
¼ Cup Balsamic Vinegar
¼ Cup Raisins
¼ Cup Walnuts (Ideally Soaked & Dehydrated)
⅓ Cup Chopped Fresh Parsley   **Serves 3-4**

Shred the beets and carrots in the food processor. Pour the shredded veggies in a salad bowl. Place the olive oil, honey, water, sea salt, and balsamic in your blender, and blend into a dressing. Pour over your salad, toss the walnuts and raisins in, and mix well. Sprinkle the fresh green herbs over the top and enjoy! So many vitamins and minerals!

Green Papaya Salad

1-2 Inches of Fresh Ginger
1 tsp Sea Salt or Tamari
2 Tbsp Agave Nectar or Honey
2 Tbsp Chopped Yellow Onion
2 Tbsp Lime or Lemon Juice
1 Medium Green Papaya (Peeled & Deseeded)
2-3 Peeled Carrots
1 Red Pepper
¼ Cup Chopped Fresh Cilantro   **Serves 2-3**

Place the ginger, salt or tamari, agave or honey, citrus juice, and onion into food processor, and process with S-blade. Remove blade and replace with shredder. Feed the green papaya, carrot, and red pepper into the shredder. Alternate to pre-mix the veggies. Transfer from processor to large mixing bowl. Add fresh cilantro and toss very well. Enjoy! Salad keeps for 3-5 days, airtight in fridge.

Celeriac Angel Hair Pasta Salad

1 Large Celeriac Vegetable
4 Tbsp Olive Oil
2 Tbsp Lemon Juice
½ tsp Sea Salt
1 Garlic Clove (crushed) or ½ tsp Garlic Powder
1 Tbsp Nutritional Yeast
½ Cup Sun-dried Tomatoes (Oil-Packed or Reconstituted)
½ Cup Pitted Kalamata Olives   **Serves 2**
Fresh Ground Coarse Black Pepper (To taste)

Wash your root vegetable and cut off the outer skin. Place the celeriac into the spiralizer. Transform the vegetable into angel hair pasta. If you don't have a spiralizer, you can also shred it. Place the celeriac noodles in a bowl. Add the remaining ingredients and toss very well.

Sweet Potato Cranberry Salad

1 Medium Sweet Potato
2 Tbsp Olive Oil
2 Tbsp Honey or Agave Nectar
1 tsp Lemon Juice
¼ tsp Apple Cider Vinegar
Pinch of Sea Salt and a Dash of Nutmeg
1 tsp Dried Parsley or 1 Tbsp Fresh
¼ Cup Pine Nuts or Sliced Almonds
½ Cup Juice Sweetened Dried Cranberries   **Serves 2-3**

Chop the ends off of the sweet potato, then rinse and peel it. Process the entire vegetable in the spiralizer for the best texture and presentation, or you can manually grate or shred in the food processor. Transfer to a small mixing bowl. If you used a spiralizer, use kitchen scissors to trim the potato into more manageable lengths. Next, blend the olive oil, honey, lemon juice, nutmeg, and vinegar in the blender. Pour over the sweet potato. Toss with parsley, cranberries, and nuts. Enjoy!

Crunchy Cabbage Salad

3 Cups Chopped or Shredded Green Cabbage
1 Cup Chopped or Shredded Purple Cabbage
½ Cup Peeled and Shredded Carrot
2 Tbsp Olive Oil
1 Tbsp Lemon Juice
½ tsp Sea Salt
2 Garlic Cloves (Crushed) or ½ tsp Garlic Powder
1 Tbsp Dill Weed (Dry or Fresh)
1 Tbsp Nutritional Yeast
Black Pepper (To taste)   **Serves 3-4**

Place cabbage and carrot in a large mixing bowl and toss until well combined. Put the remaining ingredients into the blender, blend well, and pour over the vegetables. Mix and enjoy!

Ocean Salad

2 Cups Dried Arame Seaweed
½ Cup Diced Cucumber (Deseeded)
½ Cup Diced Sweet Red Pepper (Deseeded)
3 Diced Green Onions
1 Tbsp Sesame Oil
3 Tbsp Rice Vinegar
2 Tbsp Honey or Agave Nectar
2 Tbsp Tamari
1 Tbsp Sesame Seeds   **Serves 2**
1 Tbsp Red Pepper Flakes (Optional)

Put the dried Arame to soak. While the seaweed reconstitutes, dice the cucumber, red pepper, and green onions. To make the dressing, combine the sesame oil, rice vinegar, honey, and tamari in your blender, and blend well. When the Arame is done soaking, strain the seaweed and place it in a large mixing bowl. Add diced peppers, cucumber, and onions. Pour the dressing over it and combine well. Sprinkle the sesame seeds and red pepper flakes over the top. Isn't that gorgeous? Pull out your chopsticks and get nutrified with this great salad!

❖

Shredded Zucchini and Kale Pesto Salad

2 Medium Green Zucchini
1 Bunch of Fresh Kale (Any variety)
2 Large Garlic Cloves
1 Tbsp Lemon Juice
½ tsp Sea Salt
1 Tbsp of Nutritional Yeast (Optional)
½ Cup Raw Sunflower Seeds, Cashews, Mac Nuts, or Pine Nuts
¼ Cup Olive Oil
1 Cup of Diced Tomatoes   **Serves 3-4**

Using your food processor's shredder, a manual grater, or a spiralizer, shred the zucchini. Place the shredded zucchini in your serving dish. In your food processor fitted with S-blade, place the kale, garlic, lemon juice, sea salt, and optional nutritional yeast. Blend these lively ingredients into a pesto. Once the herbs and spices are well combined, add the oil and nuts or seeds. Spread the pesto over the shredded zucchini, but do not mix. Over the top of the kale pesto layer, lay the tomatoes. Get out your fork or chopsticks and dive in. Delicious!

❖

Live Nori Rolls

Here's a fantastic live sushi recipe!

Pâté:
1 Cup Cashews (Soaked for about 2 hours) or Mac Nuts
1 Tbsp Tamari
2 Tbsp of your favorite Miso Paste
1 tsp Chopped Fresh Ginger
1 tsp Lemon Juice
1 Tbsp Olive Oil   **Serves 5-6**

Nori Sheets

Inner Ingredients:
Sprouts: Alfalfa, Clover, Radish, Sunflower, Pea Shoots
Veggies: Julienned Red Pepper, Carrot, Cucumber, Avocado
Pickled Ginger
Wasabi Paste

Pour the soaked cashews into a colander and rinse them well. Place all of the pâté ingredients into a food processor or blender and blend them very well. Add water a teaspoon at a time if needed to keep the pâté moving, but do not let it get runny!

Lay out your nori sheets with the shinier side down. Spread a 1" wide strip of pâté, evenly from side to side, on the wide edge of the nori sheet closest to you. Now, place any combination of the above listed inner ingredients over this layer. It is important to get a good ratio here. Too much pâté can make a roll feel heavy. These rolls need to be light and crunchy. So, put in lots of veggies! Roll the veggies and pâté nice and tight in the nori sheet.

Serve with Miso Soup and/or Ocean Salad for a complete meal.

Collard Wraps

Pâté:
½ Cup Sunflower Seeds (Soaked overnight)
½ Cup Pumpkin Seeds (Soaked overnight)
½ Cup Cashews (Soaked 1-2 hours) or Macadamia Nuts
¼ Cup Pure Water
2 Tbsp Tamari
1 Tbsp Agave Nectar or Honey
1 Tbsp Chopped Fresh Ginger (Optional)
2 Tbsp Lemon Juice
2 Tbsp Olive Oil
Pinch of Turmeric
Dash of Red Pepper Flakes   **Serves 5-6**

Several Collard Green Leaves

Veggies: Peeled Shredded Carrots, Jicama, or Celeriac,
Diced Sweet Pepper

Sprouts: Clover, Alfalfa, Radish, Sunflower, and/or Pea Shoots,
Chopped Cilantro

Wash the collard leaves well. Lay them on the cutting board with the coarse underside up. Remove the thickest part of the stem. This cut may be just 2-3" into the leafy part. This cut will remove the woody part of the stem and allow several inches of leaf to be used as a tortilla. Set to air dry.

To make the pâté, place the seeds and nuts into the colander and rinse well. Combine the pâté ingredients in your processor or blender. Combine well, scraping down the sides as you go.

Each collard leaf will hold approximately 1 cup of veggies depending on the size of the leaf. Choose which veggies you would like to combine, and place them into a paper towel to further dry them. Then place the veggies and diced sweet pepper into a mixing bowl. Combine the pâté and veggies. Decide how much pâté will go in each wrap. The rolls can be very filling or very light, depending on how much pâté is used. Place the sprouts over the top. Now, roll the collard shut. Ready to serve!

You are what you eat.

And you are vibrant, beautiful and

delicious!

❖

...Sprout it...

...Make it...

...Dip it...

...Eat it...

...Love it...

...Spread it...

❖

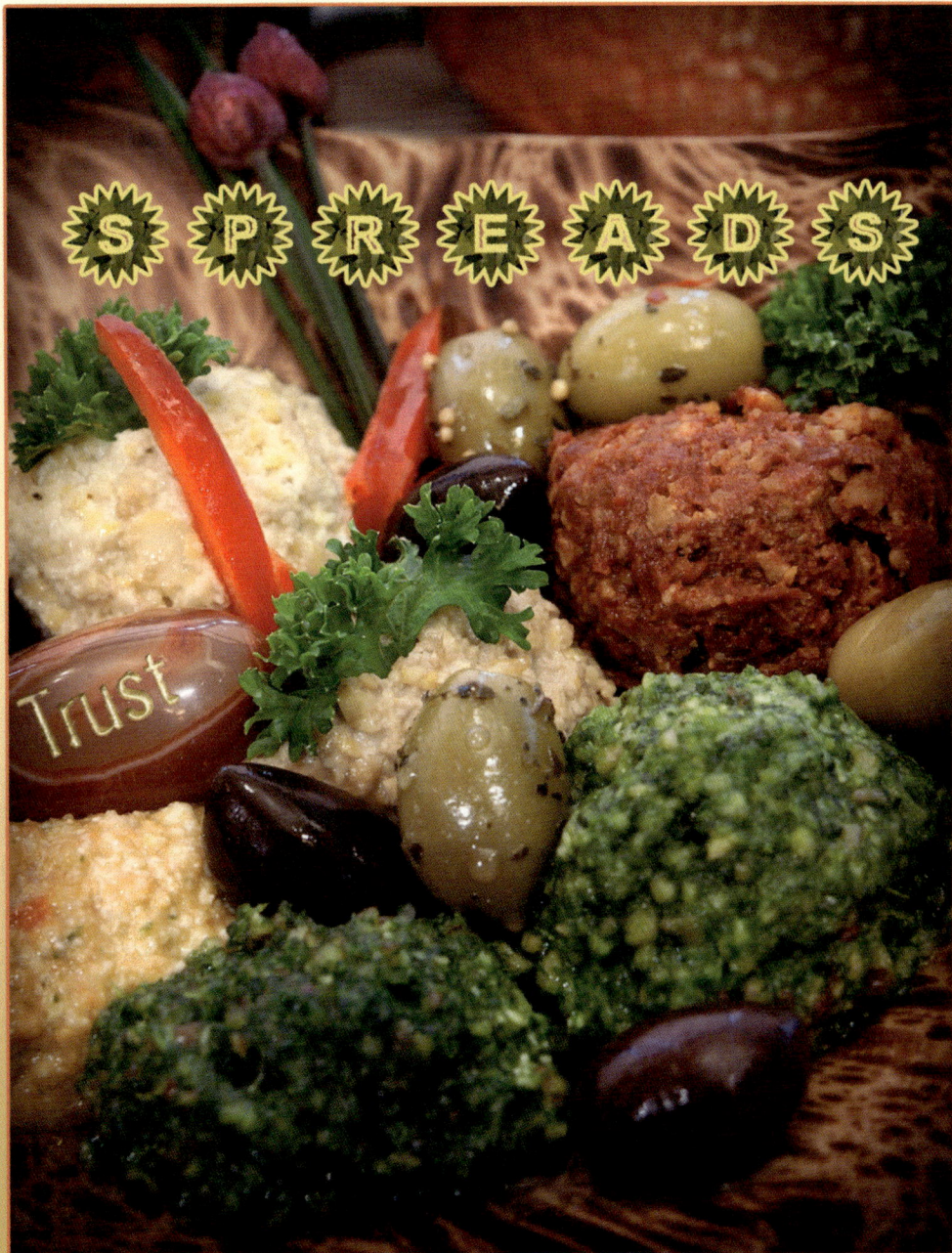

SPREADS

Trust

Jeff Eichin © 2012

Basil Pesto

6 Ounces of Fresh Basil
2 Garlic Cloves
2 Tbsp Lemon Juice
1 tsp Sea Salt
½ Cup Dry Walnuts, Pine Nuts, Cashews, Macadamia Nuts, or
    Sunflower Seeds
¼ Cup Olive Oil

Remove thick and woody stems from the basil, and wash and dry. Place the first four ingredients into the food processor and blend. Once thoroughly diced, add nuts and oil. Blend very well.

Cilantro Walnut Pesto

2 Large Bunches of Cilantro
2 Garlic Cloves
3 Tbsp Lime Juice
1 tsp Lemon Juice
2 tsp Sea Salt
1 Cup Raw Walnuts, Cashews, Mac Nuts, or Sunflower Seeds
1 Cup Ripe Avocado
¼ Cup Olive Oil

Rinse the cilantro and remove any thick, woody stems. Dry with a paper towel and place in the food processor with the first four ingredients. Blend well and then add nuts, avocado, and oil. Blend until smooth.

Kale Pesto

1 Large Bunch of Kale (Lacinato, Purple, Red, or Green)
2 Garlic Cloves
1 Tbsp Lemon Juice
½ tsp Sea Salt
½ Cup Dry Sunflower Seeds, Macadamia, Walnuts, or Pine Nuts
¼ Cup Olive

Wash, dry, and de-stem the kale. Place the first four ingredients in the food processor and blend. Once thoroughly diced, add the nuts and oil. Blend well. Serve with crackers, breads, or veggies.

Sun-Dried Tomato Pesto

1 Cup Sun-Dried Tomatoes (Dry or Packed in Olive Oil)
2 Garlic Cloves
1 Tbsp Lemon Juice
1 Tbsp Honey
½ tsp Sea Salt
½ tsp Red Pepper Flakes (Optional, for a little spice)
¼ Cup Olive Oil (And/or Oil from Packed Tomatoes)
½ Cup Dry Walnuts

If you are using dried tomatoes, soak them for at least 20 minutes and strain before making your pesto.

Place all of the ingredients into the food processor and blend until smooth. You may need to support the processor while the tomatoes are being chopped.

Creamy Carrot Spread

3 Cups Carrots (Peeled & Chopped)
1-2 Large Garlic Cloves
¼ Cup Olive Oil
1 Tbsp Lemon Juice
1 tsp Sea Salt
¼ tsp Turmeric
1 ½ Cups Cashew Nuts (Soaked for 2 hours) or Mac Nuts
¼ Cup Diced Green Onions, Chives, Basil, or Cilantro

First, let's make a carrot pesto. Place the carrots, garlic, olive oil, lemon juice, sea salt, and turmeric into the food processor. Purée these ingredients into a smooth pesto, scraping down the carrot as you go. Allow the processor to run for several minutes in all. Once the carrot is quite smooth, add the nuts. Again, allow the processor to work for you, making an evenly smooth spread. Finally, add your herbs. Process just enough to incorporate well.

Miso Tahini Spread

½ Cup of Your Favorite Miso Paste
1 Cup Raw Tahini
¼ Cup Agave Nectar, Honey, or Maple Syrup
2 Tbsp Lemon Juice
2 Inches of Fresh Raw Ginger
1 Cup fresh Water
1 Bunch Cilantro (Thoroughly Rinsed, Chopped, and Stemmed)

Wash the ginger root and chop it. Place it in the food processor and give it a pulse or two. Then, add the miso, tahini, sweetener, and lemon juice, and blend. While it is blending, add the water. Allow the ingredients to become well combined. Finally, add the cilantro. Do not overly blend the cilantro; you are adding color and flavor. Both will be lost if the cilantro is puréed too much.

Sprouted Garbanzo Hummus

2 Cups Sprouted Garbanzo Beans
½ Cup Water
2 Garlic Cloves
¼ Cup Olive Oil
2 Tbsp Lemon Juice
½ tsp Sea Salt
½ Cup Washed, Peeled, and Chopped Carrot
½ Cup Washed and Chopped Zucchini
2 Tbsp Dried or Fresh Parsley
¼ Cup Raw Tahini
¼ Cup Nutritional Yeast (Optional)

Soak the garbanzo beans overnight. Put them into the colander and rinse well. Allow these beans to sit at room temperature, rinsing several times a day for the next couple of days. They will begin to grow! Rinse them one last time and get your apron on—let's make live hummus!

Put all these fabulous ingredients in your food processor and blend until they are smooth. I find this hummus is great with savory breads and wonderful with fresh veggies such as celery, carrots, cabbage, fennel, etc. Surprise your friends with this typically-cooked classic.

For some extra adventure, try a batch with some chipotle peppers in it. Yum! I also recommend replacing the lemon juice with high quality balsamic vinegar for a very different and captivating flavor that many people love.

No-Egg Salad

2 Cups Macadamia Nuts or Cashews
¼ Cup Apple Cider Vinegar
2 Tbsp Chopped Onion
1 Garlic Clove
½ Cup Cold Pressed Olive Oil
1 tsp Sea Salt
½ tsp Turmeric
½ Cup Water
¼ Cup Chopped Celery
¼ Cup Chopped Red Pepper
¼ Cup Chopped Fresh Parsley
Sprinkle of Black Pepper or Paprika

Place the nuts, vinegar, onion, garlic, olive oil, and water into the food processor. Blend very, very well. Once the desired creaminess is achieved, fold in the celery, red pepper, and fresh parsley. Complete with your favorite sprinkle and enjoy the richness!

Mama's Nacho Spread

1 Cup Nuts
½ tsp Cumin
½ tsp Coriander
½ tsp Salt
1 Tbsp Lime Juice
2 Tbsp Olive Oil
2 Tbsp Pure Water
¼ Cup Cilantro (Chopped)
¼ Cup White or Yellow Onion (Diced)

Place the first four ingredients in the food processor. Blend these dry ingredients into fine flour. Add the lime juice, olive oil, and water, and blend well. Finally, pulse in the cilantro and onion. This is a great filling for Live Corn Tortillas (page 43)!

Fun Fennel Sensation

2 Cups Chopped Fennel (Greens & Bulb)
1 Garlic Clove
½ tsp Sea Salt
1 tsp Rice Wine Vinegar
½ Cup Olive Oil
½ Cup Soaked Nuts or Avocado

Pulse fennel until chopped. Add remaining ingredients and blend until smooth.

Sweet 'n Savory Sage Spread

1 Cup Nuts or Seeds
2 Tbsp Fresh or Dried Sage
1 tsp Raw Honey
¼ Cup Pure Water
½ tsp Sea Salt

Place seeds or nuts in food processor and process into a flour. Add remaining ingredients and blend until smooth. So savory!

Raw-Ba Ghanoush

2 Cups Eggplant
2 Garlic Cloves
½ Cup Olive Oil
¼ Cup Walnuts, Cashews, or Macadamia Nuts
¼ tsp Sea Salt
¼ Cup Lemon Juice

Slice eggplant in ¼" rounds, lightly salt them, and allow them to release water for about 20 min. Pat dry, lightly drizzle eggplant medallions with olive oil, and place in dehydrator at 115° for 4 hours. Place softened eggplant and remaining ingredients in food processor, and blend until smooth. Delish!

"Good soup is one of the prime ingredients of good living. For soup can do more to lift the spirits and stimulate the appetite than any other one dish."

"One whiff of a savory aromatic soup and appetites come to attention. The steaming fragrance of a tempting soup is a prelude to the goodness to come. An inspired soup puts family and guests in a receptive mood for enjoying the rest of the menu."

"Soup is the song of the hearth... and the home."

Louis P. De Gouy, 'The Soup Book' (1949)

SOUPS

Gazpacho

4 Tomatoes
½ of a Cucumber
2 Garlic Cloves
2 Tbsp Lemon Juice
½ tsp Sea Salt
⅓ Cup Olive Oil
1 Tbsp Honey or Agave Nectar
4 Ounces Fresh Basil
Dash of Cayenne (Optional)   **Serves 3-4**
1 Cup Water

Fresh Salsa Topping:
1 Medium Sweet Pepper
½ Small Red Onion
½ Cup Chopped Cilantro

Blend all of the ingredients, except for the topping, until quite smooth. This is the soup. Separately dice (or pulse in the processor) the topping ingredients, and mix well. Sprinkle this fresh chunky salsa over the top of the soup. This wonderful summertime soup is now ready to serve.

Cashew Cream Sauce (Topping for soup, salad, and pizza)

1 Cup Cashews (Soaked 2 hours) or Macadamia Nuts
½ tsp Sea Salt
1 Tbsp Lemon Juice
1 tsp Apple Cider Vinegar
½ Cup Water

Rinse the soaked cashews. Place all ingredients into the blender. Adjust the amount of water added according to your blender and your desired consistency. This cream can be put into a squeezable condiment dispenser and makes for a great presentation and creamy addition to many recipes.

Live Borscht (Inspired by the Boutenko Family!)

2 Cups Water
3 Beets
1" Chopped Ginger Root
2 Garlic Cloves
4 Bay Leaves
2 Cups Water
3-4 Oranges (Peeled, without seeds)
1 Tbsp Honey
2 Tbsp Apple Cider Vinegar
⅓ Cup Olive Oil
½ tsp Sea Salt   **Serves 3-4**
½ Cup Walnuts
¼ Cup Fresh Parsley

Blend the first five ingredients very well. Pour the mixture into a large bowl. Blend the next six ingredients very well. Next, add the walnuts and blend on a low speed to break them into small pieces, but not purée them. Pour this second mixture in with the first, and stir to combine. Top with fresh or dried parsley. This soup tastes great with the Cashew Cream Sauce (from the previous page).

Spicy Carrot Avocado Live Soup

2 Cups Carrot Juice
½ Medium Avocado
1 tsp Chopped Fresh Ginger
1 Tbsp Lemon Juice
1 tsp Chopped Jalapeño Pepper
1 Garlic Clove or ¼ tsp Dried
1 Tbsp Olive Oil
¼ Cup Chopped Cilantro   **Serves 2**

Blend all ingredients until completely smooth. Garnish with avocado slices, cilantro sprigs, and Cashew Cream Sauce.

Curried Cauliflower Live Soup

2 Cups Water
1 tsp Curry Powder
2 Large Ripe Tomatoes
1 Sweet Red, Orange or Yellow Bell Pepper
¼ Cup Lemon Juice
¼ Cup Olive Oil
2 Cloves Garlic
¼ Cup Chopped Sweet Onion
2 Tbsp Honey
1 tsp Sea Salt
1 Cup Chopped Cauliflower
½ Bunch Fresh Parsley   **Serves 3-4**
Fresh Ground Black Pepper to taste

Purée all ingredients into a lovely soup. This soup is as warm as a summer's day. Garnish with fresh parsley and pepper.

Sassy Salsa Soup

1 Medium Tomato
1 Bunch Fresh Cilantro
¼ Cup Chopped Yellow Onion
½ tsp Cumin
1 tsp Sea Salt
1 Garlic Clove
1 Cucumber
½ Cup Lemon Juice   **Serves 2-3**
½ Cup Avocado
1 Cup Fresh Dark Green Leaves (Chopped & Stemmed)
Pinch of Cayenne
3 Cups Pure Water

Blend all of the above ingredients into a smooth and warming soup. Top with the Cashew Cream Sauce and/or the Gazpacho Fresh Salsa Topping (page 78).

Rockin' Kelp Noodle Miso Soup

¼ Cup of your favorite Miso Paste
4 Cups of Water
12 oz. Kelp Noodles
½ tsp Garlic Powder
½ tsp Spirulina
1 Tbsp Tamari
1 tsp Sesame Seeds
1 Tbsp Dulse Flakes
2 Torn Nori Sheets   **Serves 2-3**
½ tsp Red Pepper Flakes (Optional)

Gently warm the 4 cups of water. Add the Miso paste and stir until well dissolved. Add the remaining ingredients. Gently stir to combine, and allow the ingredients to sit together, warm but not hot. It is so important to keep the temperature below 115° to keep the sea vegetables and Miso alive. Allow the soup to "stew" for ten minutes. After ten minutes, the noodles will have swelled and softened, and the soup is ready. Warm your soul. Nourish your body.

Yummy Yum Green Soup

1 Cup Spinach
1 Bunch Fresh Parsley
¼ Cup Lemon Juice
1 Medium Zucchini or Cucumber
½ Tomato
½ Red Pepper
½ tsp Sea Salt
1 Tbsp of your favorite Miso Paste
Pinch of Chipotle Powder or Cayenne   **Serves 3-4**
2-3 Cups of Pure Water

Place all ingredients into a high power blender and blend very well on medium-high. Love it!

❖

We do it all day long

In many a varied fashion

Hot, iced, or not

Creamy rich & hot

In a glass, in a mug, in a jug

At the park, in the car, or at the bar

You are what you drink,

You are...

❖

BEVERAGES

Beet Kvass

Beet Kvass is one of the most amazing beverages on the planet! It is simple to make and full of health. Kvass comes to us from the Ukraine. It is a blood tonic, liver and kidney cleanser, digestive aid, alkalizer, and cell rejuvenator.

2 Medium Beets
2 Tbsp of Raw Apple Cider Vinegar
1 tsp Sea Salt
Approximately 2 Quarts of Purified Water
One ½ Gallon Glass Jar   **Yields ½ Gallon**

Wash the beets and cut the tops and bottoms off. Chop the beets—do not grate. Place the chopped beets into the bottom of the ½ gallon glass jar. Now, add the pure water, sea salt, and apple cider vinegar. Stir. The live fermented vinegar is a catalyst of healthy fermentation for the Kvass. Cover your brew with a lid and allow the Kvass to sit at room temperature for two to three days. Then, place in the fridge (or equivalent 40° location). This will slow the fermentation and allow the beneficial lacto-bacilli to form healthy colonies. In about six days, the brew is quite yummy. Enjoy the natural effervescence and feel the undeniable health and vitality that is Beet Kvass.

Now for a little extra fun, combine your finished Beet Kvass with finished Kombucha. The flavor combination and body benefits are off the chart, not to mention the COLOR!

Yes! Yes! Yes! Just say Yes.

Kombucha

Kombucha is thought to have originated in the Far East, probably China, and has been consumed there for at least two thousand years. The first recorded use of Kombucha comes from China in 221 BC during the Tsin Dynasty. At this time it was known as "**The Tea of Immortality**".

Kombucha is an effervescent health drink. Kombucha is *alive*; full of cultures, organic acids, active enzymes, amino acids, and polyphenols. Kombucha is said to stimulate circulation and immunity, balance hormones, improve skin and digestion, cleanse the liver, alleviate arthritis, and even assist in recovery from some cancers.

The Kombucha culture looks like a pancake. It is a "S.C.O.B.Y." which stands for Symbiotic Culture of Bacteria and Yeasts. The culture is a solid mass of microorganisms.

The culture is placed in a sweet caffeinated tea, turning a jar full of sweet tea into vitamins, minerals, enzymes, and health-giving organic acids. Finished Kombucha is relatively low in caffeine and sugar, as those components are transformed into the beneficial aspects of this wonder drink.

As the Kombucha culture digests the sugar, it produces a range of organic acids like gluconic acid, lactic acid, acetic acid, butyric acid, malic acid, and usnic acid. It also contains vitamins—particularly B vitamins and vitamin C—as well as amino acids and enzymes. Then, you get the wonderful benefits of the probiotic microorganisms themselves!

You might wonder if fermenting a sweet tea with yeasts would produce an alcoholic beverage. It's a good question; the yeasts do produce alcohol, but the bacteria in the culture turn the alcohol to organic acids. Only minute quantities of alcohol, typically 1% by volume, remain in the Kombucha brew.

How to Brew Safely

To brew Kombucha, you must start with a Mother Culture. This can be done a few different ways. Ask around your community and see if anyone has a local culture. A local culture will be more adapted to your own ecosystem, and therefore the potential immune benefits will be maximized. There are also multiple sources on the internet for Kombucha. Happy Herbalist and Get Kombucha are two that I can personally vouch for. Livin' Sunshine at *LivinSunshine.com* is also happy to provide great cultures.

Brewing Kombucha at home is very serious business. Please go out of your way to keep your culture as clean as you can. Wash your glass with very hot water, sterilize it with vinegar, and only handle your culture with very clean or gloved hands.

There have been reports of adverse physical reactions to Kombucha. These may be related to unsanitary fermentation conditions, leaching of compounds from fermentation vessels, water pH that is not ideal for fermentation, or "sickly" Kombucha cultures that cannot acidify the brew. Cleanliness is important during preparation, and in most cases, the acidity of the fermented drink prevents growth of unwanted contaminants. If a culture becomes contaminated, it will most likely be seen as common mold, which is generally green, blue, or black in color. Often, novice brewers will mistake the brownish root filaments on the underside of the culture as a mold contamination.

If mold does grow on the surface of the Kombucha culture, it is best to throw out both culture and tea, and start again with a fresh Kombucha culture.

To Brew One Gallon of Kombucha:

6 Ounces of Caffeinated Tea (Green or Black- *not flavored!*)
1 Cup of Evaporated Cane Juice, Honey, or Agave Nectar
3 Quarts Purified Water
One Gallon Glass Jar
A Small Cloth (not cheesecloth) to cover mouth of jar
A Rubber Band to secure the cloth
Kombucha Culture- preferably with ⅓+ Cup Finished Brew

First, brew one quart of strong tea (pure, not flavored) in your gallon glass jar. This could be five (or so) tea bags, or ⅓ cup of loose leaf. If you are using green tea, take care not to over-steep. When over-steeped, green tea will oxidize and taste very bitter. This bitterness will transfer to your Kombucha. Brew green tea for only 3-5 minutes.

To this strong tea, add 1 cup of pure sugar, honey, or agave nectar. Stir well to dissolve. Add two quarts of pure water. Now, place the culture into the sweet tea. Cover and allow to sit in a warm, undisturbed place that is not in direct sunlight. The amount of time the brew needs to ferment varies greatly according to the room's ambient temperature. If the room is 65° or higher, the fermentation process should take about 10 days. If the temperatures are lower than 65°, the process takes longer: from two to three weeks, and sometimes even longer. The longer the brew is allowed to ferment, the more sour, vinegary, and pungent it becomes. Please harvest to your own liking.

I recommend to anyone who brews with honey to thoroughly rinse your Mother Culture (pancake-like little creature) in between brews. There is more sediment in honey than in sugar or agave. This sediment can accumulate and create an unhealthy situation if not removed periodically.

Harvest your Kombucha by removing the culture with clean or gloved hands. Set the culture aside in a container with about ⅓ cup of the Kombucha liquid. The rest is yours to enjoy!

Now start the process over again.

Place finished Kombucha in the fridge. It is now ready to be flavored.

Some Flavoring Ideas:

Make a delicious tea such as hibiscus, chai, blueberry, or mint, and add this to your finished Kombucha.

Add fresh fruit juice: Cranberry, Cherry, Pear, a Green Juice, etc.

Purée fresh ginger in fruit juice, pour through a sieve, and add to your Brew.

NOTE: It is *very* important that *no* flavor is added until the fermentation is complete. Adding flavor will likely compromise the culture and can endanger your health as well.

If you cannot brew for a while, your culture can be stored. Seal it in a jar with a lid in the fridge. Feed the culture a bit of sweet tea if you need to store it for more than a month.

Favorite Fresh Juice Combinations:

Carrot Coconut Quencher
1 Young Coconut
6 Medium Carrots

Put your carrots through a juicer. Open the young coconut and pour the water thru a sieve. Combine the two and enjoy thoroughly!

Tropical Refresh
2 Ripe Mangoes
3 Ripe Kiwi Fruits
½ Small Ripe Pineapple
½ Cup Fresh Mint
Ice

Juice the first four ingredients and pour over ice.

Beet, Apple and Celery
2 Medium Beets
2 Medium Apples
4 Stalks of Celery

Juice and drink immediately.

Tomato, Carrot, Sweet Pepper Perfection
1 Red Pepper
2 Medium Tomatoes
3 Carrots
Parsley to Taste

Prep vegetables. Juice and Enjoy!

Sweet Green Smoothies

Oh, Green Smoothies, thank the Gods and Goddesses for green smoothies and Victoria Boutenko! Green smoothies are very versatile, and recipes are great, but it is truly nice to get a hang for the ratio of fruit to greens. If you make a delicious sweet creamy smoothie, you will drink it and love it. If you make a smoothie that is chunky and bitter, you are going to feel bitter about having to drink it (and you probably won't). I like to do a three to one ratio of fruit to greens. For example, this morning, I had one banana, two dates, some brazil nut milk, and dinosaur kale in my smoothie. It was amazing... I drank two big glasses and felt great!

Here are a few recipes to get you going. From here, I feel creativity is a must. Find your fruit ratio and have fun!

Also, you need to cycle through *many* greens to achieve optimal absorption, assimilation, and integration. It will overwhelm your system if you have a large amount of one type of green every day.

Remember, make your smoothies yummy. Do not make them so bitter and chunky that you do not drink them. Especially when you are beginning, don't be shy. Use lots of fruit or honey or stevia to make it delectable.

Adding chia seeds, maca, bee pollen, or other superfoods to your smoothie is a great way to boost nutrition!

Blend the Following Green Smoothies Thoroughly:

Banana Date Perfection Blend
3 Ripe Bananas
2 Dates
1 Bunch of Dark Leafy Greens
2 Cups of Pure Water
1 tsp of Super Greens (Spirulina, Vitamineral Greens, etc.)

Parsley Cantaloupe Freshness
1 Bunch of Parsley
1 Medium Cantaloupe

Creamy Strawberry Fennel
1 Entire Green Fennel: bulb, stems and leaves
2 Cups Fresh Strawberries
1 Banana

Dreamy Tropical Blend
2 Cups Dark Greens
1-2 Dates
1 Medium Ripe Papaya (About 2 Cups)
1 Banana
2 Cups Pure Water

Roar Dinosaur Shake
1 Cucumber
Juice of 1 Lime
2 Pears
1 Bunch Dinosaur Kale Leaves

Milk is a sacred beverage.

Our life begins with milk.

Milk, sometimes referred to as "white blood," is the creamy, rich, life-sustaining beverage produced by the fertile female bodies of the world. How amazing.

When I was 20 years old, I traveled extensively in Eastern Africa. I lived with the Masai Tribe. The Masai culture revolves around their herds of goats. A person's wealth and status has much to do with their herd. It is the milk of the goats from which their abundance flows.

Most of us do not have the capacity to pasture goats and cows in our backyards. Some of us have extreme intolerance to dairy. However, with a little know-how, we can create fresh, sprouted, creamy "white blood" right in our kitchen.

Making unpasteurized nut and seed milks is so empowering, delicious, and nutritious. These milks are very versatile, from smoothie, cereal topping, beverage, to soup base, and more.

Enjoy creating sacred and healing energy.

NUT & SEED MILKS

Nut Milks

To make nut milk, start by soaking the nuts overnight. This activates their enzymes and hydrates them, making them easier to blend. However, not all nuts need this soaking. For example, brazil nuts, macadamia nuts, and hazelnuts can be made into milk without soaking. It is nice to keep some nuts like these, so you can blend up milks more spontaneously. That way, you do not always have to know seven hours ahead of time what you are going to make. **Almonds, pecans, and walnuts all have an enzyme inhibitor that makes these nuts particularly challenging to digest.** That is why it is important to soak them. Soaking de-activates these inhibitors, making the nuts more digestible.

Save your nut pulp for crackers and cakes. You can save it in the freezer to ensure freshness for when you accumulate enough to make a recipe.

Fresh nut and seed milks spoil quickly. Please use them promptly and often. They typically stay fresh and delicious for only 3 days. Sometimes, if needed, I add a teaspoon of ascorbic acid (Vitamin C) to my milk to extend its life.

Almond Milk

2 Cups Raw Almonds
½ Cup Dates or ⅓ Cup Honey, Agave Nectar, or Coconut Palm
    Syrup
½ tsp Sea Salt
4 Cups Water

Place the almonds to soak overnight, or for 7 hours. Pour the nuts into a colander and rinse. Place the soaked nuts into your blender. Add in the remaining ingredients and blend well. *Be careful not to over-blend.* You do not want to completely pulverize the nuts. You need to be able to strain the milk.

Next, pour this blend through a sieve. A nut milk bag is a wonderful tool for this. They are inexpensive, sturdy, and easy to use. If you are using a bag, put it into a jar (at least one quart) with a wide mouth. Hook the top of the nut milk bag over the mouth of the jar. Pour the mixture in. Only pour in what you can comfortably manage at a time. Squeeze the liquid through the bag into the jar. Yes, it will remind you of milking a mammal! How rich this is. Keep doing this until you have extracted all of the liquid. Refrigerate.

If you want to use a fine sieve instead of a nut milk bag, place the sieve over the jar and pour the milk through. Using a spoon, or your hand, press down on the pulp to extract as much liquid as possible. Enjoy!

Other Delicious Nut & Seed Milks

2 Cups Raw Hazelnuts, Brazil Nuts, Pecans, Macadamia Nuts, Hulled Sunflower Seeds, Hulled Pumpkin Seeds, Hemp Seeds, or any combination of the above
½ Cup Dates or ⅓ Cup Honey, Agave Nectar, or Coconut Palm Syrup
½ tsp Sea Salt
4 Cups Water

Soak the nuts or seeds overnight, for at least 7 hours. Pour them into a colander or sieve, and rinse. Place the soaked nuts or seeds into the blender. Add the remaining ingredients and blend. Pour the milk through a sieve or nut milk bag. Extract as much of the liquid as possible. Refrigerate and enjoy!

Cashew Milk

2 Cups Raw Cashews (Soaked for 2-4 hours)
½ Cup Dates or ⅓ Cup Honey, Agave, or Coconut Palm Syrup
½ tsp Sea Salt
4 Cups Water

Cashew milk is unique in that it does not need to be strained. The cashews are so porous that with a high-powered blender the consistency of this milk with the pulp is great. So, just blend thoroughly and enjoy! Store in your refrigerator.

Malted Maca Milkshake

2 Cups of any of the above Milks
2 Frozen Bananas
2 Tbsp Maca Powder
1 tsp Vanilla Extract, or Seeds from ½ of a Vanilla Bean Pod
Pinch of Sea Salt

Blend and Bliss!

Absolutely Divine Chocolate Milk

2 Cups of Any of the Above Milks
1 ½ Tbsp Cacao Powder
Pinch of Sea Salt
1 tsp Vanilla
2 Tbsp Honey, Agave Nectar, or Coconut Syrup, or ¼ Cup Dates

Blend and serve either warmed or chilled.

Sweet, Rich and Creamy Lucuma Milk

2 Cups of any of the above Milks
2 Tbsp Lucuma Powder
Pinch of Sea Salt

Blend all ingredients until thoroughly combined. Lucuma, referred to as the "Gold of the Incas," is a natural sweetener. Lucuma Powder comes from an evergreen tree in the highlands of Peru, Chile, and Ecuador. Containing Beta-Carotene, Niacin (B-vitamins), iron, and fiber, this is a sweetener that enhances flavor *and* health. In Joy!

Coconut Milk

1 Young Green Coconut
1 Mature Coconut

Open the young coconut and sieve the coconut water into the blender. Next, open the mature coconut and extract the coconut meat. Take the time and thoroughness to remove all of the woody pieces from the meat. I do this with a paring knife. Rinse the coconut meat and place into the blender. Combine the water and the meat to make milk. Magic!

When I first contemplated the raw food diet for myself, I remember saying, "If ferments aren't considered raw, I'm not doin' it!"

As a child of the Pacific Northwest, warmth and spice are a must to fend off the chilly, damp air. I just knew that if salads, room temperature soups, crackers and spreads were going to become my mainstay, I would need the heat of fermentation to warm my blood & bones.

Ferments are indeed part of the raw food diet. I recommend them daily!

FERMENTS

In lacto-fermentation, the starches and sugars in fruits and vegetables are converted to lactic acid. Lactic acid preserves foods by inhibiting the growth of bacteria. Lactobacilli, the bacteria that make this happen, are present on the surface of all plant life, and are especially abundant in leaves and roots that grow in or near the ground. Not only do these lactobacilli preserve our food, they also provide us with improved digestion and give us enhanced vitamins and probiotics. The following recipes make the most of these invisible allies.

Kimchi (Asian)

1 Medium Cabbage (Green or Napa)
1 Medium Bok Choy
1 Bunch Green Onion
1 Cup Grated Carrots
4 Garlic Cloves
½ Hot Pepper and/or 1-2 Tbsp Red Pepper Flakes
1 Tbsp Freshly Grated Ginger
2 Tbsp Sea Salt

Peel off the outer layer of cabbage as whole as you can, and set these leaves aside for later. Core and shred or chop the cabbage. Place the cabbage in a large mixing bowl. Add chopped bok choy, diced green onions, grated carrots, crushed garlic cloves, minced hot pepper, grated ginger, and sea salt. Toss. Next, pound the veggies to release their juices. This creates great texture, flavor, and fermentation. You can use a kitchen tenderizing hammer, a sturdy ladle, or even a long-neck glass bottle. Pound this salad for at least ten minutes.

Next, transfer the veggies and juices into your fermentation vessel(s). You can use any size of wide mouth glass jars, or a ceramic crock. Fill the jar or crock until it is at least one inch from the top. Press the ingredients down. The juices will rise up and cover the Kimchi. If the Kimchi is not completely covered in liquid, add enough pure water to completely submerge the veggies.

Now, place a clean whole cabbage leaf over the top of the Kimchi and press down. You may further submerge your ferment with a clean rock, the core of a cabbage, or a glass jar weighted down with water. Allow it to sit at room temperature for about 5 days, covered by a secured breathable cloth (not cheesecloth). Remove the whole leaf and any weights, then transfer into jars with lids and put them in the fridge. The fridge slows fermentation, but will not stop it. In another couple weeks, the ferment gets really delicious, and nutritious.

Sauerkraut (European)

1 Medium Green Cabbage
2 Medium Grated Carrots
2 Tbsp Caraway Seeds
2 Tbsp Sea Salt

Peel off the outer layer of cabbage as whole as you can, and set these leaves aside. Shred, grate, or chop the cabbage. Grate the carrots. Place these veggies in a large mixing bowl. Add the caraway seeds and sea salt. Mix well. With a tenderizing hammer or a long-necked glass bottle, pound the kraut for at least ten solid minutes to release the juices. Transfer everything to your fermentation vessel(s), then press the ingredients down until the juices cover them. If needed, add a little pure water to ensure that the Kraut is completely submerged. Clean the whole cabbage leaves very well and place a large leaf over the top of the kraut, pressing down. You can further submerge your ferment with a clean rock, the core of a cabbage, or a glass jar weighted down with water. Cover your ferment with a breathable cloth (not cheesecloth), and secure it with a rubber band.

Allow the ferment to sit for several days at room temperature, then remove the whole leaf and transfer it to sealed jars and into the fridge. This will slow fermentation, but not stop it. The kraut is edible immediately, but greatly improves with age.

Cortido (Latin American)

1 Large Green Cabbage (Cored and Chopped or Shredded)
2 Large Grated Carrots
1 Large Diced Onion
1 Tbsp Dried or Fresh Oregano
2 Tbsp Sea Salt
½ tsp Red Pepper Flakes

First, remove the outer leaves of the cabbage and set aside for use later. Next, in a large mixing bowl, combine all of the above ingredients. Now pound this mixture just as we did with the Sauerkraut and Kimchi. The pounding releases juices, improves texture, and provides for successful fermentation. You can use a kitchen tenderizer, a sturdy ladle, or even a long-necked glass bottle to release the juices. Pound your Cortido for ten minutes. Now, transfer the Cortido to the fermentation vessel(s). Press the ingredients down until the juices cover them. If needed, add a little water to ensure that the Cortido is completely submerged.

Take the large outer cabbage leaves, clean them very well, and use them to help submerge the veggies. Place a large leaf and weight over the top of the Cortido and press down. Cover your ferment with a secured breathable cloth (not cheesecloth).

Allow this to sit at room temperature for several days. Then transfer into quart jars with lids and put them in the fridge.

This dish is a Rawesome addition to any Southwestern or Latin meal!

Classic Dill Pickles (inspired by *Wild Fermentation*)

3-4 Pounds Small Pickling Cucumbers
⅓ Cup Sea Salt
2 Quarts Warm Pure Water
3 Heads of Fresh Flowering Dill (or 3 Tbsp Dried, or Seeds)
3 Heads of Garlic (Approximately 18 peeled & whole cloves)
1 Handful of Fresh Grape or Oak Leaves (Tannins for crunch)
1 Pinch Black Peppercorns
1 Large Whole Cabbage Leaf

Dissolve the sea salt in 2 quarts warm pure water, creating a brine. Place the garlic, dill, grape or oak leaves, and peppercorns in your fermentation vessel. Next, place the cucumbers in vertically and pour the brine over. Place the cabbage leaf over the cukes, weight it down, and cover with a cloth. Check the crock daily and skim mold from the surface. After 1-3 weeks, according to your liking, harvest your pickles. Discard the cabbage leaf, transfer to glass jars, and refrigerate.

Pickled Beets

3 Medium Beets (Peeled and Thinly Sliced)
1 White or Yellow Onion (Peeled and Thinly Sliced)
1 Garlic Clove
2 Bay Leaves
2 Strips Lemon Zest

Brine:
4 Tbsp Red Wine Vinegar
2 Cups Pure Water (Approximate amount needed to submerge)
2 tsp Sea Salt
½ tsp of Black Peppercorns

Layer the first five ingredients in a quart-sized wide mouth jar. Pour brine over, submerging. Cover with cloth, and store at room temperature for three days. Seal and transfer to fridge.

Ginger *or* Jalapeño Carrots

4 Cups Thinly Sliced Carrots (Manually or in Food Processor)
1 White or Yellow Onion, Thinly Sliced
2 Garlic Cloves

Brine:
1 Tbsp Freshly Grated Ginger or Sliced Jalapeño
¼ Cup White Wine Vinegar
2 tsp Sea Salt
2 Cups Pure Water

Layer the veggies into two quart sized wide mouth jars. Combine brine ingredients together, and pour this flavorful brine over the veggies. Add water if needed to completely submerge. Cover with cloth and leave at room temperature for three days, and then transfer to the fridge.

Pickled Zucchini & Eggplant

1 Eggplant, julienned into ½" spears
5 Zucchini (Green and/or Yellow), julienned into 1" spears

Dressing:
1 Cup Water
6-8 Cloves of Garlic
2 Tbsp Sea Salt
2 Tbsp Honey
2 Tbsp Fresh Oregano Leaves
2 Tbsp Fresh Thyme Leaves
½ Cup Apple Cider Vinegar

Place the eggplant and zucchini spears vertically into two clean quart jars. Place dressing ingredients in your blender and blend for 20 seconds. Pour this dressing over your veggies, submerging them. Cover with cloth and let sit for three days. When three days have passed, seal and transfer to cold storage.

Spicy Cranberry Relish

2 Medium Oranges (Chopped, Without Seeds & With Rind)
1 Jalapeno (Seeded & Chopped)
1 ½ Cup Raisins
½ Cup Agave Nectar or Honey
3 Cups Fresh Cranberries
1 Bunch Fresh Cilantro

Place the oranges, jalapeno, raisins, and sweetener into the food processor, and pulse until finely chopped. Next, add the fresh cranberries, and pulse a few more times. Finally, add cilantro and pulse until the desired relish consistency is achieved. Place in a glass jar in the refrigerator, sealed. This relish will keep for several weeks.

Embracing raw food is not about deprivation.

It is about creation. It is about more life,

more flavor, and more health.

❖

It is all about a sweet offering.

It is all about a sweet treat.

Creative & lovely food that feels good.

A treat should be a treat for our entire

bodies, not just our taste buds!

❖

DESSERTS

When you make a live dessert, you are the orchestrator of the ingredients. They will dance together, with you, in an alchemical sweet magic. Hold the desired texture in your mind and mouth before you begin. Guide the ingredients to where you want them to go.

The foundation of many live desserts is the nut crust.

NOTE: All of these crust recipes can be made into raw cookies. Just shape and refrigerate. Easy and Rawesome!

Simple Nut Crust

Variation One:
1 Cup Nuts of your choice
1 Cup Shredded Coconut
Pinch of Sea Salt
½ tsp Vanilla Extract, or Seeds from ¼ of a Vanilla Bean Pod
½ Cup Pitted Dates or ¼ Cup Raw Honey
1 Tbsp of Pure Water

Variation Two:
2 Cups Nuts of your choice
1 Cup of Coconut Date Rolls, Date Paste, or Pitted Dates
Pinch of Sea Salt
½ tsp Vanilla Extract, or Seeds from ¼ of a Vanilla Bean Pod
1 Tbsp of Pure Water

First, lightly grease your cake tin with coconut oil. Place the dry ingredients (nuts, salt, and optionally, coconut) into the food processor, and blend into a fine flour. Next, add the dates and vanilla. Process for at least one minute. Now, slowly, if needed, add the water to encourage the crust to bind together. Only add as much water as is absolutely necessary.

Once the above ingredients bind together, stop the appliance and transfer to the cake tin. Press the crust out to the edges. Create a flat surface that is approximately ¼" thick.

These Simple Nut Crusts can be modified and expanded on in a myriad of ways. Here are a few:

Chocolate Chip Crunch Crust
Add 2 Tbsp Raw Cacao Nibs (Sweetened or Unsweetened). Fold them in after processing.

Dark Chocolate Crust
Add ¼ Cup Raw Cacao Powder to the Simple Nut Crust recipe.

Sesame Crust
Add ¼ Cup Sesame Seeds to the Simple Nut Crust recipe, folding them in after processing. For a gourmet visual effect, you can also add 1 Tbsp Black Sesame Seeds.

Sunflower Crust
If you need to make a crust without nuts, you can substitute sunflower seeds.

Pumpkin Seed Crust
Pumpkin Seeds can also be substituted. Yes, the crust will be green in color.

The Spice for Life Crust
To the Simple Nut Crust recipe, add 1 tsp of cinnamon and a pinch of cayenne.

A Nice Anise Crust
While the nuts, coconut, and salt are blending, add a pinch of ground star anise seeds.

Citrus Zest Crust
Add 1 tsp of lemon, lime, or orange zest to the Simple Nut Crust.

The Livin' Sunshine Sweet 'n Creamy Cheesecake

Filling:
1 Cup Macadamia Nuts
1 Cup Cashews (Soaked approx. 2 hours, Rinsed & Drained)
1 Cup Coconut Meat or Yogurt (Any kind)
¾ Cup Lemon Juice
1 Cup Nut Milk (See recipes starting on page 94)
¼ Cup Raw Honey
½ Cup Agave Nectar or Coconut Palm Syrup
1 Cup Coconut Oil (Warmed in a dehydrator or double boiler)
1 tsp Vanilla Extract, or Seeds from ½ of a Vanilla Bean Pod
Pinch of Sea Salt

Begin by making a nut crust of your choice. Press this crust into an oiled 9" springform cake tin or a 12" fluted tart pan.

Blend all the ingredients until creamy and smooth. This will take several minutes. Once you have reached your desired consistency, pour the filling into the crust. Place the cake into the refrigerator. The re-hardening of the coconut oil makes the dessert firm. The cake will need several hours in the fridge.

This creamy cheesecake will keep for five days in the fridge and freezes great too.

To adorn, simply slice fresh fruit and place on top of the cake. Think of a mandala; symmetrical and repeating patterns are visually pleasing. Fresh edible flowers and herbs are lovely accents. You may also enjoy a Smooth Berry Topping.

Smooth Berry Topping

1 Cup Berries (Raspberry, Blueberry, Blackberry, etc.)
1 Cup Dates (Pitted)

Place ingredients into the blender. Blend until smooth. Spread this topping on the cheesecake.

A note on how to serve your Live Cheesecake:

There are many variables within this recipe that will affect how long it takes the cake to set up. The first variable is the temperature of the coconut oil, the second is the heat generated by blending, and the third is the cooling ability of the refrigerator.

How do you know when the cake is ready? First, give the cake tin a gentle jiggle. If the cake moves at all, it is not ready. If the cake passes the jiggle-test, then you can *gently* press a finger onto the top of the cake, in the center. If the cake is firm at this point you can be almost 100% certain that the cheesecake has set up completely. This usually takes several hours.

When the cake is done, remove it from the fridge. To remove the cake from the tin, run a spatula around the edge of the cake. Make sure you go around the entire circumference of the tin. At this point, balance the base of the tin on your dominant hand, and release the springform with your other hand. Guide the cake (still on the base) onto the counter or on to a service tray. If the cake appears soft at this stage, place it back in the refrigerator or freezer immediately. If the cake is firm, smooth the edges with your spatula. You can adorn the sides as well as the top of the cake.

Sunshine's Fruit Swirl Creamy Cheesecake

1 Livin' Sunshine Sweet 'n Creamy Cheesecake (See page 110)
1 Cup of Fresh Berries or Stone Fruit such as Apricot, Nectarine, Apricot, or Mango

Begin by making the cheesecake. Into the nut crust pour *two thirds* of the creamy, white filling. You can also place whole raspberries or sliced strawberries into this ⅔ white creamy filling in the crust. At this stage, the filling is basically liquid and you can place the fruit right in. As the cheesecake hardens around the fruit there will be whole fruits within. Lovely. Set this aside for a moment, not in the fridge yet.

To the remaining *one third* filling still in the blender, add a cup of fresh fruit and blend. You can blend until the fruit is completely smooth, or allow the fruit to be a little chunky. You can also add 1 tsp to 1 Tbsp of beet juice to accentuate the colors of a berry swirl. Or, to a fruit swirl such as mango or apricot, which are more yellow, you may choose to add 1 tsp of dried turmeric root to accentuate the color.

The cheesecake filling, with blended fruit added, is now ready to pour into the rest of the cheesecake. With confidence, pour the creamy, fruity filling into the white filling. Pour it all around and then swirl them together with a thin skewer or toothpick. Fun! Be careful not to over-swirl. You need to maintain the contrast for the fantastic visual effect. The Fruit Swirl Cheesecake is now ready to be placed into the refrigerator to set up.

Your mouth will dance with flavor and your body will dance with wholeness!

Coconut Lime Creamy Cheesecake

1 Cup Macadamia Nuts
1 Cup Cashews (Soaked approx. 2 hours, Rinsed & Drained)
1 Cup Coconut Meat or 1 Cup Yogurt (Any kind)
1 ½ Cup Coconut Milk (See recipe on page 97)
1 Cup Lime Juice
¼ Cup Raw Honey
½ Cup Agave Nectar or Coconut Palm Syrup
1 Cup Coconut Oil (Gently Melted)
1 tsp Vanilla Extract, or Seeds from ½ of a Vanilla Bean Pod
Pinch Sea Salt
1 Tbsp Spirulina

Begin with a Nut Crust. I suggest the Citrus Zest Crust!

Blend all of the above ingredients, with the exception of the Spirulina, into a creamy, delicious, sweet & tart creation. Pour two thirds into the cake crust and set aside. To the remaining one-third, add 1 Tbsp of Spirulina and blend well. Pour this healthy green creation into the white portion and swirl. Fantastic!

I recommend adorning this cake with thin slices of lime and a sprinkle of shredded coconut.

Dark Chocolate Swirl Creamy Cheesecake

Filling:
1 Cup Macadamia Nuts
1 Cup Cashews (Soaked approx. 2 hours, Rinsed & Drained)
1 Cup Coconut Meat or 1 Cup Yogurt (Any kind)
1 ½ Cup Nut Milk (See recipes starting on page 94)
2 Tbsp Lemon Juice
¼ Cup Raw Honey
½ Cup Agave Nectar or Coconut Palm Syrup
⅔ Cup Cacao Butter (Gently Warmed)
1 tsp Vanilla Extract, or Seeds from ½ of a Vanilla Bean Pod
Pinch Sea Salt

¼ Cup Raw Cacao Powder

Begin with a Nut Crust (see page 108). The Chocolate Chip Crunch Crust is a lovely accent for this recipe.

To create a Dark Chocolate Swirl Creamy Cheesecake, assemble all ingredients except the final ¼ Cup of Cacao Powder. Blend these ingredients thoroughly. Pour two-thirds of the delectable white chocolate filling into your crust. Now, add the ¼ cup raw cacao powder to the remaining filling, and blend the powder in completely. Scrape down the sides of the blender to incorporate all of the powder. If the filling becomes too thick, add 1-2 Tbsp of nut milk to maintain a good liquid consistency. Pour the dark chocolate brown into the stunning white and swirl. Amazing, right?

Top with the Chocolate Drizzle found on page 117.

There is no end to the wonderful combinations of the Cheesecake. Here are a few more fun and hopefully inspiring ideas.

White Chocolate Berry Dream Creamy Cheesecake

Filling:
1 Cup Macadamia Nuts
1 Cup Cashews (Soaked approx. 2 hours, Rinsed & Drained)
1 Cup Coconut Meat or 1 Cup Yogurt (Any kind)
2 Tbsp Lemon Juice
2 Cups Nut Milk (See recipes starting on page 94)
¼ Cup Raw Honey
½ Cup Agave Nectar or Coconut Palm Syrup
½ Cup Cacao Butter (Gently Warmed)
¼ Coconut Oil (Gently Warmed)
1 tsp Vanilla Extract, or Seeds from ½ of a Vanilla Bean Pod
Pinch Sea Salt
1 Cup Fresh or Thawed Frozen Berries

1 tsp – 1 Tbsp Beet Juice (Optional, for color)

Begin with a Nut Crust (from page 108). The Dark Chocolate Nut Crust is great with this recipe.

Combine all ingredients, except for the 1 cup of fresh or frozen berries, in your food processor or blender. Blend for several minutes, until very smooth. Pour two-thirds of this delectable creamy creation into the Dark Chocolate Crust. You have the option of placing some whole berries into this smooth white filling. As it cools, the cheesecake will harden around these berries, enhancing the beauty and pleasure of your creation.

To the remaining one-third filling still in your blender, add the 1 cup of berries. You can blend them until fully smooth or leave them slightly chunky, *chef's choice*. You can also add 1 tsp–1 Tbsp of beet juice to accentuate the colors of the berry swirl. Once you have your desired consistency, pour this one-third into the white filling and now swirl with a skewer or toothpick.

Consider topping with the Chocolate Drizzle on page 117.

Aromatic Maca Chai Tea Creamy Cheesecake

1 Cup Macadamia Nuts
1 Cup Cashews (Soaked approx. 2 hours, Rinsed & Drained)
1 Cup Coconut Meat or 1 Cup Yogurt (Any kind)
1 ¼ Cup Chai Tea (Strong)
¾ Cup Nut Milk (See recipes starting on page 94)
¼ Cup Raw Honey
½ Cup Agave Nectar or Coconut Palm Syrup
¾ Cup Coconut Oil (Gently Warmed)
1 tsp Vanilla Extract, or Seeds from ½ of a Vanilla Bean Pod
1 Tbsp Cinnamon
1 tsp Nutmeg
½ tsp Cardamom
Pinch Sea Salt

¼ Cup Raw Maca Powder
¼ Cup Raw Cacao Powder

This cake is truly decadent. It's so many people's favorite, including my daughter. Begin with a Nut Crust (see page 108). I suggest the Dark Chocolate Crust with 2 Tbsp raw cacao nibs folded in.

After making a sensational crust, blend all of the above ingredients, *except* for the Maca and Cacao Powders, very well. Pour two-thirds of the creamy filling into your crust, and then add the Maca and Cacao Powders to the remaining one-third. Blend until well incorporated. You may have to add a small amount (1-2 tsp) of Chai or Nut Milk to keep a good liquid consistency. Pour this darker brown portion of the Cheesecake into the lighter brown batch, and swirl.

Decadent Chocolate Drizzle

Here's a Chocolate Topping Recipe that will harden in the fridge and be an amazing topping with a snap.

¼ Cup Raw Cacao Butter
¼ Cup First Cold Press Coconut Oil
2 Tbsp Raw Honey, Coconut Palm Syrup, or Agave Nectar
2 Tbsp Raw Cacao Powder

Gently melt the butter and oil together. You can do this in the dehydrator, double boiler, or oven. The goal is to keep the temperature below 105°. Next, add the sweetener to the melted butter. Allow them to warm together, achieving the same temperature and viscosity. Once this is done, whisk them together. Add the remaining ingredients and whisk until *completely* smooth. Allow this to cool and thicken a bit, then pour into a squirt bottle and drizzle over your cake. You can also pour it into a plastic bag, make a tiny hole in the corner, and squeeze the chocolate sauce through this small hole. Once the Chocolate Drizzle has been applied, place the dessert back in the fridge to allow the Decadent Chocolate Drizzle to harden.

Raw Cacao or Carob Avocado Mousse

Mousse Filling
1 Cup Ripe Avocado
¾ Cup Coconut Oil (Gently Warmed)
¼ Cup Raw Honey
¼ Cup Agave Nectar or Coconut Palm Syrup
¼ Cup of Nut Milk (See recipes starting on page 94)
1 tsp Vanilla Extract, or Seeds from ½ of a Vanilla Bean Pod
¼ Cup Raw Carob or Cacao Powder
Pinch of Sea Salt

Begin with a Nut Crust (see recipe on page 108). Because the texture of the Avocado Mousse is so delectable, I suggest using the Simple Nut Crust recipe so as not to introduce any distracting elements. You could also use the Dark Chocolate Crust recipe.

Let's create the mousse filling. Place the avocado into your food processor or blender. Add the gently warmed coconut oil, sweetener, nut milk, vanilla, salt, and either the carob or cacao powder. Combine this amazing mixture. Process for a few minutes and be sure to scrape down the sides to get the smoothest mousse possible. Remove the mousse from the processor and spread it out into the pie crust. Refrigerate and serve once the cake has set (see tips on page 111).

Once the mousse has set, it can be topped with the Coconut Cream Frosting on the next page. It is, of course, amazing when topped with fresh fruit.

This is such a healthful recipe because of all the great Omega fatty oils in the mousse. When you serve this mousse, you and your guests will feel treated and nourished. What a loving combination!

Live Key Lime Pie

Key Lime Filling
1 Large Ripe Avocado
¾ Cup Lime Juice
¾ Cup Coconut Oil (Gently Melted)
¼ Cup Raw Honey
¼ Cup Agave Nectar or Coconut Palm Syrup
¼ Cup Nut Milk or Coconut Milk (See recipes from page 94)
1 tsp Vanilla Extract, or Seeds from ½ of a Vanilla Bean Pod
Pinch Sea Salt

First, make a nut crust (see recipes starting on page 108). The Citrus Zest Crust is especially great with this recipe.

Now, combine the filling ingredients in the blender or food processor. Process them until *completely* smooth and then pour them into your pie crust. Use a spatula to help transfer and smooth. Place in the fridge to set up. Once your filling has set, you may top with this fantastic Coconut Cream Frosting.

Coconut Cream Frosting
1 ½ Cup Coconut Milk (See recipe on page 97)
1 ½ Cup Soaked Cashews or Macadamia Nuts
1 Cup Coconut Meat or 1 Cup Yogurt (Any kind)
¼ Cup Raw Honey
½ Cup Agave Nectar or Coconut Palm Syrup
1 Cup Coconut Oil (Gently Melted)
1 tsp Vanilla Extract, or Seeds from ½ of a Vanilla Bean Pod
2 Tbsp Lemon Juice
Pinch of Sea Salt

Place all ingredients into blender and blend until *completely* smooth. Pour this into a container and put in the fridge to set. Frost your mousse with an artist's stroke. Alternatively, you can pour the frosting right on to the set-up mousse for a very smooth finish. Then place into the "raw food oven," also known as "the fridge," to finish.

The Simplest Fruit Pies

Find new health and new ease in making a simple fruit pie. How exciting, right?

Begin with a Simple Nut Crust (see recipes on page 108). When making the Simplest Fruit Pies, I suggest the Simple, Sesame, Pumpkin, Sunflower, Spice for Life, Nice Anise, and the Citrus Zest Crusts.

For a *Smooth* Fruit Torte:
1 Cup Fresh or Frozen Fruit
1 Cup Dates
2 Tbsp Psyllium Husk
Splash of Lemon Juice

Blend ingredients very well and then spread out evenly on your crust. Allow the pie to set up in the refrigerator for a short time.

For a *Chunky* Fruit Filling:
1 Cup Fresh or Frozen Fruit
½ Cup Fresh, Frozen, or Dried Berries
⅓ Cup Fruit Juice
1 tsp Cinnamon
Pinch of Nutmeg and/or Cardamom
Tiny pinch of Sea Salt

Place the fruits into a bowl and combine well with the spices and juice. Allow them to sweetly marinate for ten minutes. Then, use a straining spoon to place the fruit into the pie shell or into the individual pie shells. Garnish with edible flowers or fresh herbs such as mint or spearmint.

Add a delectable crumble topping:
1 Cup of the Nut of Your Choice *or* 1 Cup of a Sprouted Cereal
    Blend (Starting on page 52)
¼ Cup Honey, Agave Nectar, or Coconut Palm Syrup
Pinch of Sea Salt
¼ Cup Gently Melted Coconut Oil or Coconut Butter

Place these lovely ingredients into the processor and pulse until well combined. Sprinkle evenly over your Simple Fruit Pie.

And To Top it All Off:
It is very enjoyable to add a dollop of the Coconut Cream Frosting from page 119, the Cream Cheese Frosting from page 125, or the Mac Nut Glaze on page 25.

Thank you for co-creating a universe

where we can all shine like the sun!

Pulp Cakes

The base for these hearty cakes is either nut or fruit pulp from making fresh nut milks or fresh juice. This pulp, along with coconut date rolls, extra virgin coconut oil, sea salt, and vanilla, make for an extra healthy and amazing combination for person and palette.

The basic cake assembly is the same for all of the following pulp cake recipes. We will combine the ingredients for the cake batter, mixing by hand, food processor, or tabletop mixer. Be careful not to over-mix. The batter needs to remain light. It will become dense with excessive mixing.

Now, when I say "mix by hand," I do not mean with a spoon. I am referring to both of your beautiful, strong hands in the mixing bowl, squeezing and massaging these fantastic ingredients into cake form. Alternatively, you can use a tabletop mixer, or pulse small batches together in the food processor.

Once the ingredients are well incorporated, yet not over-mixed, place half of the batter into the bottom of the cake tin. Smooth this layer out until it is level. Over the top of that layer, pour half of the frosting. Place this layer and the remaining frosting into the fridge or freezer until it is firm. Once the frosting has set up, press the remaining cake batter over that. Finally, spread out the remaining frosting and other adorning fruits.

This is the basic how-to for Pulp Cakes. They are a bit labor intensive, but are a special treat to enjoy: wonderful for a special occasion, and full of health and beauty. Just like you!

Strawberry Cake with Coconut Cream Frosting

1 9" Springform Cake Tin
2 Cups Coconut Date Rolls or Date Paste (Room temperature)
¾ Cup Coconut Oil (Gently Warmed)
1 tsp Vanilla Extract, or Seeds from ½ of a Vanilla Bean Pod
1 tsp Sea Salt
2 Cups Nut Pulp from making Nut Milks (Recipe on page 94)
2 Cups Shredded Coconut
¼ Cup Lemon Juice
1 Tbsp Beet Juice (For Color)
2 Cups Strawberries (Topped & Quartered)
One batch of Coconut Cream Frosting (See pages 119 or 125)

Place the 2 cups of dates in a large mixing bowl, and gently mash them with a fork to form a light paste. It is important to have the dates at room temperature because cold dates will cause the coconut to re-harden prematurely. Combine this date paste with the nut pulp, coconut oil, vanilla, salt, lemon juice, and beet juice in a large mixing bowl. You can do this in your food processor, tabletop mixer, or with your hands. Be *very* careful not over-mix so that the cake batter does not become dense or firm; the batter should remain light. Once the ingredients are fully incorporated, fold in the strawberries. Place half of this batter into the base of your cake tin. Spread it out evenly to the sides, and place in the refrigerator as you make the frosting. The remaining batter should stay out while you make the frosting.

Pour half of the coconut cream frosting over the bottom portion of your cake. Put this in the fridge or freezer to set up. Pour the remaining half into a container and place in the refrigerator. When the frosting on the first layer is firm, add the second layer of cake. Spread the remaining frosting over this layer. Adorn with fresh strawberries and spearmint leaves.

Sweet 'n Tart Lemon Poppy Seed Dream Cake

1 9" Springform Cake Tin
2 Cups Coconut Date Rolls or Date Paste (Room Temperature)
¾ Cup Coconut Oil (Warmed in a Dehydrator or Double-boil)
1 tsp Vanilla Extract, or Seeds from ½ of a Vanilla Bean Pod
1 tsp Sea Salt
2 Cups Nut Pulp (From making Nut Milks starting on page 94)
2 Cups Shredded Coconut
¾ Cup Lemon Juice
¼ Cup Poppy Seeds

In a large mixing bowl, place 2 cups of coconut date rolls. Use a fork to carefully mash the dates to form a light paste. Next, combine this date paste with the remaining ingredients. You can work these ingredients together by hand, by pulsing your food processor, or with a tabletop mixer. Spread half of the batter evenly into your cake tin and put in the fridge.

Lemon Cream Frosting

1 Cup Soaked Cashews or Macadamia Nuts
1 Cup Coconut Meat or 1 Cup Yogurt (Any kind)
1 ¼ Cup Nut Milk (Recipes starting on page 94)
¾ Cup Lemon Juice
¼ Cup Raw Honey
½ Cup Agave Nectar or Coconut Palm Syrup
½ tsp Vanilla Extract, or Seeds from ¼ of a Vanilla Bean Pod
Pinch Sea Salt
1 ¼ Cup Coconut Oil
½ tsp Turmeric Powder (Optional, for color)

Blend all ingredients until smooth. Once thoroughly creamed, pour half over the bottom portion of your cake. Put this in the fridge or freezer to set up. Pour the remaining half into a container and place in the refrigerator. When the frosting on the first layer is firm, add the second layer of cake. Over this layer, spread the remaining frosting. Adorn with fresh fruit.

Classic Carrot Cake

1 9" Springform Cake Tin
4 Cups Carrot Pulp (From about 4 lbs. Peeled & Juiced Carrots)
2 Cups Coconut Date Rolls or Date Paste (Room Temperature)
2 Cups Sunflower Seeds
2 ½ Cups Shredded Coconut
¼ Cup Fresh Orange Juice
¼ Cup Coconut Palm Syrup or Raw Honey
2 Tbsp Coconut Oil
3 tsp Cinnamon
2 tsp Nutmeg

Place all ingredients into a large mixing bowl and combine either by hand, tabletop mixer, or food processor. While you mix, remember to keep the cake light. Season to taste. Place half of this cake batter into the cake tin and refrigerate.

Classic Cream Cheese Frosting

1 ½ Cups Soaked Cashews or Macadamia Nuts
1 Cup Coconut Meat or 1 Cup Yogurt (Any kind)
1 ½ Cup Nut or Seed Milk (Starting on page 94)
¼ Cup Raw Honey
½ Cup Agave Nectar or Coconut Palm Syrup
1 Cup Coconut Oil
¼ Cup Lemon Juice
1 Tbsp Apple Cider Vinegar
Pinch of Sea Salt
1 tsp Vanilla Extract, or Seeds from ½ of a Vanilla Bean Pod

Blend all ingredients until completely smooth. Pour half of the frosting onto the first layer of cake. Place this base layer of cake into the fridge or freezer until the frosting is firm. Pour the remaining half into a container and place in the refrigerator to firm up. Once the frosting has set on the base layer, add the next layer of cake. Remove the cake from the springform and use a spatula to frost the top and sides. Top with fresh fruit.

Raw Cacao Cake

1 9" Springform Cake Tin
4 Cups Carrot Pulp (From about 4 lbs. Peeled & Juiced Carrots)
2 Cups Sunflower Seeds (Finely ground)
2 Cups Shredded Coconut
2 Cups Coconut Date Rolls
¾ Cup Raw Tahini
1 ½ Cup Raw Cacao Powder
2 tsp Vanilla Extract, or Seeds from a Whole Vanilla Bean Pod
Pinch of Sea Salt

In a large mixing bowl, place the 2 cups of coconut date rolls. Use a fork to carefully mash the dates to form a light paste. Next, combine this date paste with the remaining ingredients. You can work these ingredients together by hand, by pulsing a food processor, or with a tabletop mixer. Be sure not to over-mix; keep the cake as light as possible. Spread half of the batter evenly into your cake tin, and place in the fridge. The remaining batter can stay on the countertop while we make the frosting.

Raw Cacao Avocado Cream Frosting

1 Ripe Avocado
¼ Cup Coconut Oil (Warmed in dehydrator or in a double boil)
¼ Cup Raw Honey, Agave Nectar, or Coconut Palm Syrup
¼ Cup Raw Cacao Powder

Blend until entirely smooth. Spread this frosting over the bottom layer of cake. Place in the fridge or freezer to set up. Once firm, add the top layer of cake. Dress the entire cake with the remaining frosting.

Add a layer of fun and beauty with the Decadent Chocolate Drizzle on page 117.

Bliss on top of bliss on top of bliss!

Simple & Delicious Raw Sweet Treats

Deep Dark Decadent Chocolate Cake

2 Cups Raw Walnuts
½ Cup Raw Cacao Powder
Pinch of Sea Salt
2 Cups Coconut Date Rolls
1 tsp Vanilla Extract, or Seeds from ½ of a Vanilla Bean Pod
1-2 Tbsp of Pure Water (Only as necessary to bind)

This simple cake is basically a crust recipe that makes for an incredibly satisfying dessert. Place your dry ingredients into the food processor. Pulse and process into a flour. Add the dates, vanilla, and water (as necessary). Once the nuts, dates, and cacao have uniformly combined, stop the processor. Press half of the batch evenly into the base of a cake tin. Over this, place a smooth layer of fruit frosting. Then add your final layer of cake, and adorn.

Smooth Fruit Frosting

1 Cup Fruit
1 Cup Dates

Place ingredients into the blender and blend until smooth.

Strawberries Served With Dipping Chocolate

2 Pints of Beautiful Fresh Organic Strawberries
1 Recipe of Raw Cacao Avocado Cream Frosting (See page 126)

Clean the strawberries and choose only the most attractive berries for your creation. Allow them to air dry on a towel. Slice the berries in half and arrange in a beautiful Mandala on a dish. Place the frosting in a dish in the center. Easy, quick, and oh-my-goodness good!

Raw Halvah

2 Cups Sesame Seeds
1 Cup Raisins
¼ Cup Raw Honey, Agave Nectar, or Coconut Palm Syrup
Pinch of Sea Salt

Place sesame seeds and salt into food processor and process into a flour. Add the sticky sweetener and raisins. Process to combine. Remove and place on a tray. Press into a ½" thick rectangle. Cut into bars and sprinkle with whole sesame seeds.

Raw Puddings

Place all ingredients into the blender. Blend until completely smooth. Pour into your serving dishes and place them in the fridge to set up. I suggest topping with fresh fruit.

Raw Chocolate Pudding
1 Cup Nuts
½ Cup Honey, Pitted Dates, Agave, or Coconut Palm Syrup
2 Cups Water
1 tsp Vanilla Extract, or Seeds from ½ of a Vanilla Bean Pod
½ tsp Sea Salt
2 Tbsp Psyllium Husk Powder
2 Tbsp Coconut Oil (Gently Melted)
¼ Cup Raw Cacao Powder

Lemon Pudding
1 Cup Nuts
½ Cup Honey, Pitted Dates, Agave, or Coconut Palm Syrup
2 Cups Water
1 tsp Vanilla Extract, or Seeds from ½ of a Vanilla Bean Pod
2 Tbsp Psyllium Husk Powder
2 Tbsp Coconut Oil (Gently Melted)
3 Tbsp Lemon Juice
1 tsp Lemon Rind

Strawberry Pudding
1 Cup Nuts
½ Cup Honey, Pitted Dates, Agave, or Coconut Palm Syrup
2 Cups Water
1 tsp Vanilla Extract, or Seeds from ½ of a Vanilla Bean Pod
½ tsp Sea Salt
2 Tbsp Psyllium Husk Powder
2 Tbsp Coconut Oil (Gently Melted)
2 Tbsp Lemon Juice
½ tsp Lemon Rind
1 Cup Strawberries

You Are Invited…

You are invited to use these recipes. Add them to your wonderful life. Enjoy the clarifying feeling of changing the ratio of cooked to uncooked foods in your life. Being 75% Raw, or so, is lighter, more healthy, very creative, very colorful, and very fun. Have fun with this. I sure do. I enjoy being a raw foodist, but not being dogmatic about it. I am free to enjoy health and balance. And so are you!